Dr. Jonathan A Play In Three Acts

Winston Churchill

[ZHINGOORA BOOKS]

This edition is published by
Zhingoora Books.

zhingoora_books@yahoo.com

CONTENTS

PREFACE

DR. JONATHAN

ACT I

ACT II

ACT III

PREFACE

This play was written during the war. But owing to the fact that several managers politely declined to produce it, it has not appeared on any stage. Now, perhaps, its theme is more timely, more likely to receive the attention it deserves, when the smoke of battle has somewhat cleared. Even when the struggle with Germany and her allies was in progress it was quite apparent to the discerning that the true issue of the conflict was one quite familiar to American thought, of self-determination. On returning from abroad toward the end of 1917 I ventured into print with the statement that the great war had every aspect of a race with revolution. Subliminal desires, subliminal fears, when they break down the censor of law, are apt to inspire fanatical creeds, to wind about their victims the flaming flag of a false martyrdom. Today it is on the knees of the gods whether the insuppressible impulses for human freedom that come roaring up from the subliminal chaos, fanned by hunger and hate, are to thrash themselves out in anarchy and insanity, or to take an ordered, intelligent and conscious course. Of the Twentieth Century, industrial democracy is the watchword, even as political democracy was the watchword of the two centuries that preceded it. Economic power is at last realized to be political power. No man owns himself, no woman owns herself if the individual is not economically free. Perhaps the most encouraging omen of the day is the fact that many of our modern employers, and even our modern financiers and bankers seem to be recognizing this truth, to be growing aware of the danger to civilization of its continued suppression. Educators and sociologists may supply the theories; but by experiment, by trial and error,—yes, and by prayer,—the solution must be found in the practical domain of industry.

DR. JONATHAN

ACT I

SCENE: The library of ASHER PINDAR'S house in Foxon Falls, a New England

    village of some three thousand souls, over the destinies of which

    the Pindars for three generations have presided. It is a large,

    dignified room, built early in the nineteenth century, with white

    doors and gloss woodwork. At the rear of the stage,—which is the

    front of the house,—are three high windows with small, square panes

    of glass, and embrasures into which are fitted white inside

    shutters. These windows reach to within a foot or so of the floor;

    a person walking on the lawn or the sidewalk just beyond it may be

    seen through them. The trees bordering the Common are also seen

    through these windows, and through a gap in the foliage a glimpse of

    the terraced steeple of the Pindar Church, the architecture of which

    is of the same period as the house. Upper right, at the end of the

    wall, is a glass door looking out on the lawn. There is another

    door, lower right, and a door, lower left, leading into ASHER

    PINDAR'S study. A marble mantel, which holds a clock and certain

    ornaments, is just beyond this door. The wall spaces on the right

    and left are occupied by high bookcases filled with respectable

    volumes in calf and dark cloth bindings. Over the mantel is an oil painting of the Bierstadt school, cherished by ASHER as an

inheritance from his father, a huge landscape with a self-conscious

sky, mountains, plains, rivers and waterfalls, and two small figures

of Indians—who seem to have been talking to a missionary. In the

spaces between the windows are two steel engravings, "The Death of

Wolfe on the Plains of Abraham" and "Washington Crossing the

Delaware!" The furniture, with the exception of a few heirlooms,

such as the stiff sofa, is mostly of the Richardson period of the

'80s and '90s. On a table, middle rear, are neatly spread out

several conservative magazines and periodicals, including a

religious publication.

TIME: A bright morning in October, 1917,

GEORGE PINDAR, in the uniform of a first lieutenant of the army,

enters by the doorway, upper right. He is a well set up young man

of about twenty-seven, bronzed from his life in a training camp, of

an adventurous and social nature. He glances about the room, and

then lights a cigarette.

ASHER PINDAR, his father, enters, lower right. He is a tall,

strongly built man of about sixty, with iron grey hair and beard.

His eyes are keen, shadowed by bushy brows, and his New England features bear the stamp of inflexible "character." He wears a black

"cutaway" coat and dark striped trousers; his voice is strong and

resonant. But he is evidently preoccupied and worried, though he

smiles with affection as he perceives GEORGE. GEORGE'S fondness for

him is equally apparent.

GEORGE. Hello, dad.

ASHER. Oh, you're here, George.

GEORGE (looking, at ASHER). Something troubling you?

ASHER (attempting dissimulation). Well, you're going off to France, they've only given you two days' leave, and I've scarcely seen anything of you. Isn't that enough?

GEORGE. I know how busy you've been with that government contract on your hands. I wish I could help.

ASHER. You're in the army now, my boy. You can help me again when you come back.

GEORGE. I want to get time to go down to the shops and say goodbye to some of the men.

ASHER. No, I shouldn't do that, George.

GEORGE (surprised). Why not? I used to be pretty chummy with them, you know,—smoke a pipe with them occasionally in the noon hour.

ASHER. I know. But it doesn't do for an employer to be too familiar with the hands in these days.

GEORGE. I guess I've got a vulgar streak in me somewhere, I get along with the common people. There'll be lots of them in the trenches, dad.

ASHER. Under military discipline.

GEORGE (laughing). We're supposed to be fighting a war for democracy. I was talking to old Bains yesterday,—he's still able to run a lathe, and he was in the Civil War, you know. He was telling me how the boys in his regiment stopped to pick blackberries on the way to the battle of Bull Run.

ASHER. That's democracy! It's what we're doing right now—stopping to pick blackberries. This country's been in the war six months, since April, and no guns, no munitions, a handful of men in France—while the world's burning!

GEORGE. Well, we won't sell Uncle Sam short yet. Something is bothering you, dad.

ASHER. No—no, but the people in Washington change my specifications every week, and Jonathan's arriving today, of all days.

GEORGE. Has Dr. Jonathan turned up?

ASHER. I haven't seen him yet. It seems he got here this morning. No telegram, nothing. And he had his house fixed up without consulting me. He must be queer, like his father, your great uncle, Henry Pindar.

GEORGE. Tell me about Dr. Jonathan. A scientist,—isn't he? Suddenly decided to come back to live in the old homestead.

ASHER. On account of his health. He was delicate as a boy. He must have been about eight or nine years old when Uncle Henry left Foxon Falls for the west,—that was before you were born. Uncle Henry died somewhere in Iowa. He and my father never got along. Uncle Henry had as much as your grandfather to begin with, and let it slip through his fingers. He managed to send Jonathan to a medical school, and it seems that he's had some sort of a position at Johns Hopkins's—research work. I don't know what he's got to live on.

GEORGE. Uncle Henry must have been a philanthropist.

ASHER. It's all very well to be a philanthropist when you make more than you give away. Otherwise you're a sentimentalist.

GEORGE. Or a Christian.

ASHER. We can't take Christianity too literally.

8

GEORGE (smiling). That's its great advantage, as a religion.

ASHER. George, I don't like to say anything just as you're going to fight for your country, my boy, but your attitude of religious skepticism has troubled me, as well as your habit of intimacy with the shop hands. I confess to you that I've been a little afraid at times that you'd take after Jonathan's father. He never went to church, he forgot that he owed something to his position as a Pindar. He used to have that house of his overrun with all sorts of people, and the yard full of dirty children eating his fruit and picking his flowers. There's such a thing as being too democratic. I hope I'm as good an American as anybody, I believe that any man with brains, who has thrift, ought to rise—but wait until they do rise. You're going to command men, and when you come back here into the business again you'll be in a position of authority. Remember what I say, if you give these working people an inch, they'll take all you have.

GEORGE (laying his hand on ASHER's shoulder). Something is worrying you, dad. We've always been pretty good pals, haven't we?

ASHER. Yes, ever since you were a little shaver. Well, George, I didn't want to bother you with it—today. It seems there's trouble in the shops,—in our shops, of all places,—it's been going on for some time, grumbling, dissatisfaction, and they're getting higher wages than ever before—ruinous wages. They want me to recognize the union.

GEORGE. Well, that beats me. I thought we were above the labour-trouble line, away up here in New England.

ASHER (grimly). Oh, I can handle them.

GEORGE. I'll bet you can. You're a regular old war horse when you get started. It's your capital, it's your business, you've put it all at the disposal of the government. What right have they to kick up a row now, with this war on? I must say I haven't any sympathy with that.

ASHER (proudly). I guess you're a real Pindar after all, George.

(Enter an elderly maid, lower right.)

MAID. Timothy Farrell, the foreman's here.

(Enter, lower right, TIMOTHY, a big Irishman of about sixty, in

working clothes.)

TIMOTHY. Here I am, sir. They're after sending word you wanted me.

GEORGE (going up to TIMOTHY and shaking his hand warmly). Old Timothy! I'm glad to get sight of you before I go.

TIMOTHY. And it's glad I am to see you, Mr. George, before you leave. And he an officer now! Sure, I mind him as a baby being wheeled up and down under the trees out there. My boy Bert was saying only this morning how we'd missed the sight of him in the shops this summer. You have a way with the men, Mr. George, of getting into their hearts, like. I was thinking just now, if Mr. George had only been home, in the shops, maybe we wouldn't be having all this complaint and trouble.

GEORGE. Who's at the bottom of this, Timothy? Rench? Hillman? I thought so. Well, they're not bad chaps when you get under their skins.

(He glances at his wrist watch)

Let me go down and talk with them, dad,—I've got time, my train doesn't leave until one thirty.

ASHER (impatiently, almost savagely). No, I'll settle this, George, this is my job. I won't have any humoring. Come into my study, Timothy.

TIMOTHY, shaking his head, follows ASHER out of the door, left.

After a moment GEORGE goes over to the extreme left hand corner of

the room, where several articles are piled. He drags out a kit bag,

then some necessary wearing apparel, underclothes, socks, a sweater,

etc., then a large and rather luxurious lunch kit, a pin cushion.

with his monogram, a small travelling pillow with his monogram, a linen toilet case embroidered in blue, to hang on the wall—these

last evidently presents from admiring lady friends. Finally he

brings forth a large rubber life preserving suit. He makes a show

of putting all these things in the bag, including the life-

preserving suit; and reveals a certain sentiment, not too deep, for

the pillow, the pincushion and the toilet case. At length he strews

everything over the floor, and is surveying the litter with mock

despair when a girl appears on the lawn outside, through one of the

windows. She throws into the room a small parcel wrapped in tissue

paper, and disappears. GEORGE picks up the parcel and looks

surprised, and suddenly runs out of the door, upper right. He

presently returns, dragging the girl by the wrists, she resisting.

MINNIE FARRELL is about twenty one, with black hair and an abundant

vitality. Her costume is a not wholly ineffective imitation of

those bought at a great price at certain metropolitan

establishments. A string of imitation pearls gleams against her

ruddy skin.

MINNIE. Cut it out, George! (Glancing around apprehensively.) Say, if your mother was to find me here she'd want to send me up to the reformatory (she frees herself).

GEORGE. Where the deuce did you blow in from? (Regarding her with admiration.) Is this the little Minnie Farrell who left Foxon Falls two years ago? Gee whiz! aren't we smart!

MINNIE. Do you like me? I'm making good money, since the war.

GEORGE. Do I like you? What are you doing here?

MINNIE. My brother Bert's out there—he ain't working today. Mr. Pindar sent for father, and we walked up here with him. Where is he?

GEORGE (nodding toward the study). In there. But what are you doing, back in Foxon Falls?

MINNIE. Oh, visiting the scenes of my childhood.

GEORGE (tearing open the tissue paper from the parcel). Did you make these for me? (He holds up a pair of grey woollen wristlets.)

MINNIE. Well, I wanted to do something for a soldier, and when I heard you was going to France I thought you might as well have 'em.

GEORGE. How did you hear I was going?

MINNIE. Bert told me when I came home yesterday. They say it's cold in the trenches, and nothing keeps the hands so warm as wristlets. I know, because I've had 'em on winter mornings, early, when I was going to work. Will you wear 'em, George?

GEORGE. Will I wear them! (He puts then on his wrists.) I'll never take them off till the war's over.

MINNIE (pleased). You always were a josher!

GEORGE. Tell me, Minnie, why did you run away from me two years ago?

MINNIE. Run away from you! I left because I couldn't stand this village any longer. It was too quiet for me.

GEORGE. You're a josher! You went off while I was away, without telling me you were going. And then, when I found out where you were and hustled over to Newcastle in my car, you turned me down hard.

MINNIE. You didn't have a mortgage on me. There were plenty of girls of your own kind at that house party you went to. I guess you made love to them, too.

GEORGE. They weren't in the same class with you. You've got the ginger.

MINNIE. I've still got the ginger, all right.

GEORGE. I thought you cared for me.

MINNIE. You always had the nerve, George.

GEORGE. You acted as if you did.

MINNIE. I'm a good actor. Say, what was there in it for me?—packing tools in the Pindar shops, and you the son of my boss? You didn't want nothing from me except what all men want, and you wouldn't have wanted that long.

GEORGE. I was crazy about you.

MINNIE (her eyes falling on the travelling pillow and the pincushion; picking theron: up in turn). I guess you told them that, too.

GEORGE (embarrassed). Oh, I'm popular enough when I'm going away. They don't care anything about me.

MINNIE (indicating the wristlets). You don't want them,—I'll give 'em to Bert.

GEORGE. No, you won't.

MINNIE. I was silly. But we had a good time while it lasted,—didn't we, George?

(She evades him deftly, and picks up the life-preserving suit.)

What's this?—a full dress uniform?

GEORGE. When a submarine gets you, all you've got to do is to jump overboard and blow this—

(He draws the siren from the pocket and starts to blow it, but she

seizes his hand.)

—and float around until a destroyer picks you up.

(Takes from another pocket a metal lunch box.)

This is for pate de foie gras sandwiches, and there's room in here—

(Indicating another pocket.)

—for a bottle of fizz. Come along with me, Minnie, ship as a Red Cross

nurse, and I'll buy you one. The Atlantic wouldn't be such a bad place,

with you,—and we wouldn't be in a hurry to blow the siren. You'd look

like a peach in a white costume, too.

MINNIE. Don't you like me in this?

GEORGE. Sure, but I'd like that better.

MINNIE. I'd make a good nurse, if I do say it myself. And I'd take good care of you, George,—as good as any of them.

(She nods toward the pillow and pincushion.)

GEORGE. Better!

(He seizes her hands and attempts to draw her toward him.)

You used to let me!

MINNIE. That ain't any reason.

GEORGE. Just once, Minnie,—I'm going away.

MINNIE. No. I didn't mean to come in here—I just wanted to see what you looked like in your uniform.

(She draws away from him, just as Dr. JONATHAN appears in the

doorway, lower right.)

Goodbye, George.

(She goes out through the doorway, upper right.)

(DR. JONATHAN may be almost any age,—in reality about thirty five.
His head is that of the thinker, high above the eyes. His face
bears evidence in its lines of years of labour and service, as well
as of a triumphant struggle against ill health. In his eyes is a
thoughtful yet illuminating smile, now directed toward GEORGE who,
when he perceives him, is taken aback,)

DR. JONATHAN. Hello! I was told to come in here,—I hope I'm not intruding.

GEORGE. Not at all. How—how long have you been here?

DR. JONATHAN. Just long enough to get my bearings. I came this morning.

GEORGE. Oh! Are you—are you Dr. Jonathan?

DR. JONATHAN. I'm Jonathan. And you're George, I suppose.

GEORGE. Yes. (He goes to him and shakes hands.) I'm sorry to be leaving just as you come.

DR. JONATHAN. I'll be here when you return.

GEORGE. I hope so (a pause). You won't find Foxon Falls a bad old town.

DR. JONATHAN. And it will be a better one when you come back.

GEORGE. Why do you say that?

DR. JONATHAN (smiling). It seems a safe conjecture.

(Dr. JONATHAN is looking at the heap of articles on the floor.)

GEORGE (grinning, and not quite at ease). You might imagine I was embarking in the gent's furnishing business, instead of going to war. (He picks up the life-preserving suit.) Some friend of mother's told her about this, and she insisted upon sending for it. I don't want to hurt her feelings, but I can't take it, of course.

(He rolls it up and thrusts it under the sofa, upper left.)

You won't give me away?

DR. JONATHAN. Never!

GEORGE. Dad ought to be here in a minute, he's in there with old Timothy Farrell, the moulder foreman. It seems that things are in a mess at the shops. Rotten of the men to make trouble now—don't you think?—when the country's at war! Darned unpatriotic, I say.

DR. JONATHAN. I saw a good many stars in your service flag as I passed the office door this morning.

GEORGE. Yes. Over four hundred of our men have enlisted. I don't understand it.

DR. JONATHAN. Perhaps you will, George, when you come home.

GEORGE. You mean—

(GEORGE is interrupted by the entrance, lower right, of his mother,

AUGUSTA PINDAR. She is now in the fifties, and her hair is turning

grey. Her uneventful, provincial existence as ASHER'S wife has

confirmed and crystallized her traditional New England views, her

conviction that her mission is to direct for good the lives of the

less fortunate by whom she is surrounded. She carries her knitting

in her hand,—a pair of socks for GEORGE. And she goes at once to

DR. JONATHAN.)

AUGUSTA. So you are Jonathan. They told me you'd arrived—why didn't you come to us? Do you think it's wise to live in that old house of your father's before it's been thoroughly heated for a few days?

DR. JONATHAN (taking her hand). Oh, I'm going to live with the doors and windows open.

AUGUSTA. Dear me! I understand you've been quite ill, and you were never very strong as a child. I made it my business to go through the house yesterday, and I must say it looks comfortable. But the carpenters and plumbers have ruined the parlour, with that bench, and the sink in the corner. What are you going to do there?

DR. JONATHAN. I'm having it made into a sort of laboratory.

AUGUSTA. You don't mean to say you intend to do any work!

DR. JONATHAN. Work ought to cure me, in this climate.

AUGUSTA. You mean to practise medicine? You ought to have consulted us. I'm afraid you won't find it remunerative, Jonathan,—but your father was impractical, too. Foxon Falls is still a small place, in spite of the fact that the shops have grown. Workmen's families can't afford to pay big fees, you know.

DR. JONATHAN (smiling). I know.

AUGUSTA. And we already have an excellent physician here, Dr. Senn.

DR. JONATHAN. I shan't interfere with Dr. Senn.

GEORGE (laying his hand on AUGUSTA's shoulder: apologetically). Mother feels personally responsible for every man, woman and child in Foxon Falls. I shouldn't worry about Dr. Jonathan if I were you, mother, I've got a notion he can take care of himself.

AUGUSTA (a little baffled by DR. JONATHAN's self-command, sits down and begins to knit). I must get these socks finished for you to take with you, my dear. (To DR. JONATHAN) I can't realize he's going! (To GEORGE) You haven't got all your things in your bag! Where's the life-preserving suit I sent for?

GEORGE (glancing at DR. JONATHAN). Oh that's gone, mother.

AUGUSTA. He always took cold so easily, and that will keep him warm and dry, if those terrible Germans sink his ship. But your presents, George! (To DR. JONATHAN:) Made for him by sisters of his college friends.

GEORGE (amused but embarrassed). I can't fit up a section of the trenches as a boudoir.

AUGUSTA. Such nice girls! I wish he'd marry one of them. Who made you the wristlets? I hadn't seen them.

GEORGE (taking of the wristlets and putting them in his bag). Oh, I can't give her away. I was—just trying them on, to see if they fitted.

AUGUSTA. When did they come?

GEORGE (glancing at DR. JONATHAN). Er—this morning.

(Enter ASHER and TIMOTHY from the study, left. ASHER is evidently

wrought up from his talk with TIMOTHY.)

ASHER. Remember, Timothy, I rely on sensible men like you to put a stop to this nonsense.

AUGUSTA. Asher, here's Jonathan.

ASHER. Oh! (He goes up to DR. JONATHAN and takes his hand, though it is quite evident that his mind is still on the trouble in the shops). Glad to see you back in Foxon Falls, Jonathan. I heard you'd arrived, and would have dropped in on you, but things are in a muddle here just now.

DR. JONATHAN. Not only here, but everywhere.

ASHER. You're right. The country's going to the dogs. I don't know what will straighten it out.

DR. JONATHAN. Intelligence, open-mindedness, cooperation, Asher.

ASHER (arrested: looking at him). Hum!

DR. JONATHAN (leaving him and going up to TIMOTHY). You don't remember me, Timothy?

TIMOTHY. Sure and I do, sir,—though you were only a little lad. You mind me of your father,—your smile, like. He was the grand, simple man! It's happy I am to see you back in Foxon Falls.

DR. JONATHAN. Yes, I've been ordered to the rear.

TIMOTHY. The rear, is it? I'm thinking we'll be fighting this war in Foxon Falls, too.

DR. JONATHAN. Yes, much of it will be fought behind the battle lines.

AUGUSTA. You think the Germans will come over here?

DR. JONATHAN. No, but the issue is over here already.

(DR. JONATHAN picks up her ball of wool, which has fallen to the

floor.)

AUGUSTA (looking at him apprehensively: puzzled). Thank you, Jonathan.

(She turns to TIMOTHY, who has started toward the door, lower right)

Wait a moment, Timothy, I want to ask you about your children. What do you hear from Minnie? I always took an interest in her, you know,—especially when she was in the tool packing department of the shops, and I had her in my Bible class. I appreciated your letting her come,—an Irishman and a Catholic as you are.

TIMOTHY. The Church has given me up as a heathen, ma'am, when I married your cook, and she a Protestant.

AUGUSTA. I've been worried about Minnie since she went to Newcastle. She has so much vitality, and I'm afraid she's pleasure loving though she seemed to take to religion with her whole soul. And where's Jamesy?

TIMOTHY. Jamesy, is it? It's gone to the bad entirely he is, with the drink. He left the shops when the twelve-hour shifts began—wherever he's at now. It's home Minnie came from Newcastle yesterday, ma'am, for a visit,—she's outside there now, with Bert,—they walked along with me.

19

AUGUSTA. Bring them in, I want to see them,—especially Minnie. I must say I'm surprised she should have come home without calling on me.

TIMOTHY. I'll get them, ma'am.

(He goes out of the door, upper right. GEORGE, who has been

palpably ill at ease during this conversation, now makes for the

door, lower right.)

AUGUSTA. Where are you going, my dear?

GEORGE (halting). I thought I'd look around and see if I'd forgotten anything, mother.

AUGUSTA. Stay with us,—there's plenty of time.

(TIMOTHY returns through the doorway, upper right, with BERT, but

without MINNIE.)

TIMOTHY. It's disappeared entirely she is, ma'am,—here one minute and there the next, the way with young people nowadays. And she's going back to Newcastle this afternoon, to her job at the Wire Works.

AUGUSTA. I must see her before she goes. I feel in a measure responsible for her. You'll tell her?

TIMOTHY. I'll tell her.

AUGUSTA. How are you getting along, Bert?

BERT. Very well, thank you, Mrs. Pindar.

(The MAID enters, lower right.)

MAID. Miss Thorpe wishes to speak with you, ma'am.

AUGUSTA (gathering up her knitting). It's about the wool for the Red Cross.

(Exit, lower right.)

GEORGE (shaking hands with BERT). Hello, Bert,—how goes it?

BERT. All right, thank you, lieutenant.

GEORGE. Oh, cut out the title.

(BERT FARRELL is about twenty three. He wears a brown flannel shirt

and a blue four-in-hand tie, and a good ready-made suit. He holds

his hat in front of him. He is a self-respecting, able young Irish

American of the blue-eyed type that have died by thousands on the

battle fields of France, and whose pictures may be seen in our

newspapers.)

ASHER. You're not working today, Bert?

BERT. I've left the shops, Mr. Pindar,—I got through last night.

ASHER. Left the shops! You didn't say anything about this, Timothy!

TIMOTHY. No, sir,—you have trouble enough today.

ASHER (to BERT). Why did you leave?

BERT. I'm going to enlist, Mr. Pindar,—with the Marines. From what I've heard of that corps, I think I'd like to join it.

ASHER (exasperated). But why do you do a thing like this when you must know I need every man here to help turn out these machines? And especially young men like you, good mechanics! If you wanted to serve your country, you were better off where you were. I got you exempted—(catching himself) I mean, you were exempted from the draft.

BERT. I didn't want to be exempted, sir. More than four hundred of the boys have gone from the shops, as well as Mr. George here, and I couldn't stand it no longer.

21

ASHER. What's Mr. George got to do with it? The cases are different.

BERT (stoutly). I don't see that, Mr. Pindar. Every man, no matter who he is, has to decide a thing like this for himself.

GEORGE. Bert's right, dad.

ASHER. You say he's right, when you know that I need every hand I can get to carry out this contract?

GEORGE. He's going to make a contract, too. He's giving up all he has.

ASHER. And you approve of this, Timothy?

TIMOTHY. Sure, I couldn't stop him, Mr. Pindar! And it's proud I am of him, the same as you are of Mr. George, that he'd be fighting for America and liberty.

ASHER. Liberty! License is what we're getting now! The workman thinks he can do as he pleases. And after all I've done for my workmen,—building them a club house with a piano in it, and a library and a billiard table, trying to do my best to make them comfortable and contented. I pay them enough to buy pianos and billiard tables for themselves, and you tell me they want still higher wages.

TIMOTHY. They're saying they can go down to the shipyards, where they'd be getting five dollars and thirty cents a day.

ASHER. Let them go to the shipyards, if they haven't any sense of gratitude! What else do they say?

TIMOTHY. That you have a contract, sir, and making millions out of it.

ASHER. What can they know about my profits?

TIMOTHY. It's just that, sir,—they know nothing at all. But they're saying they ought to know, since things is different now, and they're working for the war and the country, the same as yourself.

ASHER. Haven't I established a system of bonuses, to share my profits with the efficient and the industrious?

TIMOTHY. They don't understand the bonuses,—how you come by them. Autocracy is the word they use. And they say you put up a notice sudden like, without asking them, that there'd be two long shifts instead of three eight-hour ones. They're willing to work twelve hours on end, for the war, they say, but they'd want to be consulted.

ASHER. What business is it of theirs?

TIMOTHY. Well, it's them that has to do the hard work, sir. There was a meeting last night, I understand, with Rench and Hillman and a delegate come from Newcastle making speeches, the only way they'd get their rights would be for you to recognize the union.

ASHER. I'll never recognize a union! I won't have any outsiders, meddlers and crooks dictating my business to me.

TIMOTHY. I've been with you thirty years, come December, Mr. Pindar, and you've been a good employer to me. I don't hold with the unions—you know it well, sir, or you wouldn't be asking me advice. I'm telling you what they're saying.

ASHER. I didn't mean to accuse you,—you've been a good and loyal employee— that's why I sent for you. Find out what their game is, and let me know.

TIMOTHY. It's not a detective I am, Mr. Pindar. I'm a workman meself. That's another thing they're saying, that you'd pay detectives to go among them, like workingmen.

ASHER (impatiently). I'm not asking you to be a detective,—I only want you to give me warning if we are to have a strike.

TIMOTHY. I've warned you, sir,—if it's only for the sake of beating the Germans, the dirty devils.

GEORGE (turning to BERT). Well, here's wishing you luck, Bert, and hoping we'll meet over there. I know how you feel,—you want to be in it, just as I do.

ASHER (turning). Perhaps I said more than I meant to, Bert. I've got to turn out these machines in order that our soldiers may have shrapnel to fight with, and what with enlistments and the determination of unscrupulous workmen to take advantage of the situation, I'm pretty hard pressed. I can't very well spare steady young men like you, who have too much sense and too much patriotism to mix yourselves up with trouble makers. But I, too, can understand your feeling,—I'd like to be going myself. You might have consulted me, but your place will be ready for you when you come back.

BERT. Thank you, sir. (He turns his hat over in his hands.) Maybe it would be fair to tell you, Mr. Pindar, that I've got a union card in my pocket.

ASHER. You, Timothy Farrell's son!

TIMOTHY. What's that? And never a word to me!

BERT (to TIMOTHY). Why wouldn't I join the union? I took out the card this morning, when I see that that's the only way we'll get what's coming to us. We ain't got a chance against the employers without the union.

TIMOTHY. God help me, to think my son would join the union,—and he going to be a soldier!

BERT (glancing at GEORGE). I guess there'll be other union men in the trenches besides me.

ASHER. Soldier or no soldier, I'll never employ any man again who's joined a union.

GEORGE (perturbed). Hold on, dad!

ASHER. I mean what I say, I don't care who he is.

BERT (who retains his self-possession). Excuse me, Mr. Pindar, but I'd like to ask you a question—I've heard the men talking about this in the shops. You don't like it if we go off to—fight, but if we join the union you fire us, no matter how short-handed you are.

ASHER. It's a principle with me,—I won't have any outside agency dictating to me.

BERT. But if it came to recognizing the union, or shutting down?

ASHER. I'd shut down tomorrow.

(GEORGE, who sees the point, makes a gesture as if about to

interrupt.)

BERT. That's what I'm getting at, Mr. Pindar. You say you'd shut down for a principle, whether the government gets the machines or not. And the men say they'd join the union for a principle, whether the government gets the machines or not. It looks to me as if both was hindering the war for a principle, and the question is, which principle is it that agrees best with what we're fighting for?

ASHER. No man joins a union for a principle, but for extortion. I can't discuss it,—I won't!

BERT. I'm sorry, sir.

(He turns to go out, lower right.)

GEORGE (overtaking him and grasping his hand). So long, Bert. I'll look you up, over there!

BERT (gazing at him). All right, Mr. George.

GEORGE. Goodbye, Timothy. Don't worry about the boy.

TIMOTHY. It's proud I am to have him go. Mr. George,—but I can't think why he'd be joining the union, and never telling me.

(He stands for a moment troubled, glancing at ASHER, torn between

loyalty to his employer and affection for his son. Then he goes out

slowly, upper right. All the while DR. JONATHAN has stood in the

rear of the room, occasionally glancing at GEORGE. He now comes

forward, unobtrusively, yet withal impressively.)

ASHER. I never expected to hear such talk from a son of Timothy Farrell,—a boy I thought was level-headed. (To DR. JONATHAN) What do you think of that? You heard it.

DR. JONATHAN. Well, he stated the issue, Asher.

ASHER. The issue of what?

25

DR. JONATHAN. Of the new century.

GEORGE. The issue of the new century

ASHER. You're right, we've got to put these people down. After the war they'll come to heel,—we'll have a cheap labour market then.

DR. JONATHAN. Humanity has always been cheap, but we're spending it rather lavishly just now.

ASHER, You mean that there will be a scarcity of labour? And that they can continue to blackmail us into paying these outrageous wages?

DR. JONATHAN. When you pay a man wages, Asher, you own him,—until he is turned over to somebody else.

ASHER (puzzled, a little suspicious for the first time). I own his labour, of course.

DR. JONATHAN. Then you own his body, and his soul. Perhaps he resents being regarded as a commodity.

ASHER. What else is labour?

DR. JONATHAN. How would you like to be a commodity?

ASHER. I? I don't see what that has to do with it. These men have no consideration, no gratitude, after the way I've treated them.

DR. JONATHAN. Isn't that what they object to?

ASHER. What?

DR. JONATHAN. To being treated.

ASHER. Object to kindness?

DR. JONATHAN. To benevolence.

ASHER. Well, what's the difference?

DR. JONATHAN. The difference between self-respect and dependence.

ASHER. Are—are you a Socialist?

DR. JONATHAN. NO, I'm a scientist.

(ASHER is standing staring at him when the MAID enters, lower

right.)

MAID. Your long distance call to Washington, sir.

ASHER. Very well.

(As he starts to go out he halts and looks at DR. JONATHAN again,

and then abruptly leaves the room, lower right, following the MAID.)

GEORGE (who has been regarding DR. JONATHAN: after a moment's hesitation). You seem to think there's something to be said for the workman's attitude, Dr. Jonathan.

DR. JONATHAN. What is his attitude, George?

GEORGE. Well, you heard Bert just now. I thought he had poor old dad on the hip when he accused the employer of holding up the war, too. But after all, what labour is after is more money, isn't it? and they're taking advantage of a critical situation to get it. And when they get money, most of them blow it in on sprees.

DR. JONATHAN. George, what are you going to France to fight for?

GEORGE. Germany's insulted our flag, murdered our people on the high seas and wants to boss the world.

DR. JONATHAN (smiling). The issue, then, is human freedom.

GEORGE. Sure thing!

DR. JONATHAN. And you think every man and woman in this country is reasonably free?

GEORGE. Every man can rise if he has the ability.

DR. JONATHAN. What do you mean by rise?

GEORGE. He can make money, set up for himself and be his own boss.

DR. JONATHAN. In other words, he can become free.

GEORGE (grinning). I suppose that's one way of putting it.

DR. JONATHAN. Money gives him freedom, doesn't it? Money gave you yours,—to go to school and college until you were twenty four, and get an education,—such as it was.

GEORGE. Such as it was!

DR. JONATHAN. Money gave you the choice of engaging in an occupation in which you could take an interest and a pride, and enabled you occasionally to go on a spree, if you ever went on a spree, George.

GEORGE. Once in awhile.

DR. JONATHAN. But this craving for amusement, for excitement and adventure isn't peculiar to you and me. Workingmen have it too,—and working girls.

GEORGE. You're a wise guy, I guess.

DR. JONATHAN. Oh no,—not that! But I've found out that you and I are not so very different from Timothy Farrell and his children,—Bert and Jamesy and—Minnie.

GEORGE (startled, and looking around to follow DR. JONATHAN'S glance toward the windows). What do you know about them?

DR. JONATHAN. Oh, nothing at first hand. But I can see why Bert's going to the war, and why Jamesy took to drink, and why Minnie left Foxon Falls.

GEORGE. The deuce you can!

DR. JONATHAN. And so can you, George. When you get back from France you will know what you have been fighting for.

GEORGE. And what's that?

DR. JONATHAN. Economic freedom, without which political freedom is a farce. Industrial democracy.

GEORGE. Industrial democracy! Well, it wasn't included in my education at Harvard.

DR. JONATHAN. Our education begins, unfortunately, after we leave Harvard,— with Bert and Jamesy and Minnie. And here's Minnie, now!

GEORGE (hastily). I'll beat it! Mother wants to talk to her.

DR. JONATHAN (his hand on GEORGE'S arm). No,—wait.

(Enter, lower right, AUGUSTA, followed by MINNIE FARRELL. MINNIE,

AUGUSTA'S back being turned toward her, gives GEORGE a wink, which

he acknowledges, and then glances toward DR. JONATHAN. AUGUSTA,

with her knitting, seats herself in an armchair. Her attitude is

somewhat inquisitorial; her tone, as she addresses MINNIE, non-

committal. She is clearly offended by MINNIE'S poise and good-

natured self-assertion.)

AUGUSTA. You remember Mr. Pindar, Minnie.

MINNIE (demurely). Glad to meet you again, Mr. Pindar. I hear you're going off to the war. Well, that's great.

GEORGE (squeezing her hand; she winces a little). Oh, yes,-I remember Minnie.

AUGUSTA. And this is Dr. Jonathan Pindar.

MINNIE (who has been eyeing DR. JONATHAN as a possible enemy; with reserve). Glad to meet you, I'm sure.

DR. JONATHAN (smiling at her as he takes her hand). The pleasure is—mutual.

MINNIE (puzzled, but somewhat reassured). Glad to meet you.

DR. JONATHAN. I've come to live in Foxon Falls. I hope we'll be friends.

MINNIE. I hope so. I'm going back to Newcastle this afternoon, there's nothing doing here.

DR. JONATHAN. Would you stay, if there were something doing?

MINNIE. I—I don't know. What would I be doing here?

AUGUSTA (disapprovingly, surveying, MINNIE'S costume). I don't think I should have recognized you, Minnie.

MINNIE. City life agrees with me, Mrs. Pindar. But I needed a little rest cure, and I came to see what the village looked like.

DR. JONATHAN. A sort of sentimental journey, Minnie.

MINNIE (flashing a look at GEORGE, and another at DR. JONATHAN). Well, you might call it that. I get you.

AUGUSTA. Minnie, what church do you attend in Newcastle?

MINNIE. Well, I haven't got a seat in any particular church, Mrs. Pindar.

AUGUSTA. I didn't expect you to go to the expense of getting a seat. I hope you delivered the letter our minister gave you to the minister of the First Church in Newcastle.

MINNIE. No, I didn't, Mrs. Pindar, and that's the truth. I never went near a church.

AUGUSTA (drily). It's a pity you ever went to Newcastle, I think.

MINNIE. It's some town! Every time you ride into it you see a big sign, "Welcome to Newcastle, population one hundred and six thousand, and growing every day. Goodbye, and thank you!"

AUGUSTA (knitting). You drive about in automobiles!

MINNIE. Oh, sometimes I get a joy ride.

AUGUSTA. It grieves me to hear you talk in this way. I knew you were pleasure loving, I thought I saw certain tendencies in you, yet you seemed to realize the grace of religion when you were in my Bible class. Your brother Jamesy took to drink—

MINNIE. And I took to religion. You meant to be kind, Mrs. Pindar, and I thank you. But now I know why Jamesy took to drink—it was for the same reason I took to religion.

AUGUSTA (scandalized). Minnie!

MINNIE. We were both trying to be free, to escape.

AUGUSTA. To escape? From what?

MINNIE (with a gesture indicating futility). I guess it would be pretty hard to get it across to you, Mrs. Pindar. But I was working ten hours a day packing tools in your shops, and all you gave me when the whistle blew was—Jesus.

  (A pause: GEORGE takes a step toward her.)

Jamesy took to drink, and I took to Jesus. I'm not saying anything against Him. He had His life, but I wanted mine. Maybe He would have understood.

  (Turning impulsively toward DR. JONATHAN.)

I've got a hunch that you understand.

AUGUSTA. Minnie, I can't let you talk about religion in this way in my presence.

MINNIE. I'm sorry, Mrs. Pindar, I knew it wasn't no use to come and see you,—I told father so.

AUGUSTA. I suppose, if you're determined to continue this life of—(she catches herself) I can't stop you.

MINNIE (flaring up). What life? Don't worry about me, Mrs. Pindar,—I get twenty five dollars a week at the Shale Works making barb wire to trip up the Huns with,— enough to get nice clothes—(she glances down at her dress) and buy good food, and have a good time on the side.

AUGUSTA (whose conceptions of what she believes to be MINNIE's kind are completely upset). You still work?

MINNIE. Work! Sure I work. I wouldn't let any man get a strangle hold on me. And I don't kick at a little overtime, neither. I'm working for what he's going to fight for—(indicating GEORGE) it ain't for myself only, but for everybody that ain't been free, all over the world. (To DR. JONATHAN.) Ain't that right? (She does not wait for his nod of approval.) I was just saying this morning—(she looks toward GEORGE and catches herself)—I've been wishing all along I could do more—go as a nurse for some of the boys.

AUGUSTA. A nurse!

MINNIE (to DR. JONATHAN). If I was a man, I'd have been a doctor, like you. Sick people don't bother me, I give myself to 'em. Before mother died, when she was sick, she always said I'd ought to have been a nurse. (A pause.) Well, I guess I'll go along. The foreman only give me a couple of days off to see the old home town.

GEORGE. Hold on, Minnie.

MINNIE. What is it?

GEORGE (to AUGUSTA). Minnie and I are old friends, mother.

AUGUSTA. Old friends?

GEORGE. Yes. I knew her—very well before she went away from Foxon Falls, and I went to Newcastle and took her out for a drive in my car.

MINNIE (vehemently). No, you never.

GEORGE. Why do you deny it?

MINNIE. There's nothing to it.

AUGUSTA (aghast). George!

GEORGE. Well, it's true. I'm not ashamed of it, though Minnie appears to be.

MINNIE (on the verge of tears). If you wasn't ashamed, why didn't you tell, her before? I'm not ashamed of it, neither. It was natural.

AUGUSTA (after a pause, with a supreme effort to meet the situation). Well, I suppose men are different. But there's no excuse for you, after all I tried to do for you.

MINNIE. Thank God men are different!

(AUGUSTA rises. The ball of wool drops to the floor again, and DR.

JONATHAN picks it up.)

GEORGE. Mother, I'd like to tell you about it. You don't understand.

AUGUSTA. I'm afraid I do understand, dear.

(As she leaves the room, with dignity, GEORGE glances appealingly at

DR. JONATHAN.)

DR. JONATHAN (going up to MINNIE and taking her hand). Do you think you'd have time to drop in to see me, Minnie, before your train goes?

MINNIE (gazing at him; after a moment). Sure! I guess I'd like to talk to you.

DR. JONATHAN. It's the little white house across the Common.

MINNIE. Oh, I know, that's been shut up all these years.

DR. JONATHAN. And is open now again.

(He goes out, lower right, and there is a brief silence as the two

look after him.)

MINNIE. Say, who is he?

GEORGE. Why, he's a cousin of mine—

MINNIE. I don't mean that. He's somebody, ain't he?

GEORGE. By jingo, I'm beginning to think he is!

(They stand gazing at one another.)

MINNIE (remembering her grievance: passionately). Now you've gone and done it—telling your mother we were friends.

GEORGE. But we are—aren't we? You couldn't expect me to keep quiet, under the circumstances.

MINNIE. She thinks I'm not fit to talk to you. Not that I care, except that I was fond of her, she's been good to me in her way, and I felt real bad when I went off to Newcastle with the letter to the minister I never laid eyes on. She'll believe—you know what she'll believe,—it'll trouble her. She's your mother, and you're going away. You might have kept still.

GEORGE. I couldn't keep still. What would you have thought of me?

MINNIE. It don't make any difference what I'd have thought of you.

GEORGE. It makes a difference to me, and it makes some difference what I think of myself. I seem to be learning a good many things this morning.

MINNIE. From him?

GEORGE: You mean Dr. Jonathan?

MINNIE. Yes.

GEORGE (reflecting). I don't know. I'm learning them from you, from everybody.

MINNIE. Maybe he put you wise.

GEORGE. Well, I don't feel wise. And seeing you again this morning brought it all back to me.

MINNIE. You were only fooling.

GEORGE. I began that way,—I'll own up. But I told you I'd never met a girl like you, you're full of pep—courage—something I can't describe. I was crazy about you,—that's straight,—but I didn't realize it until you ran off, and then I went after you,—but it was no good! I don't claim to have been square with you, and I've been thinking—well, that I'm responsible.

MINNIE. Responsible for what?

GEORGE. Well-for your throwing yourself away down there at Newcastle. You're too good.

MINNIE (with heat). Throwing myself away?

GEORGE. Didn't you? Didn't you break loose?—have a good time?

MINNIE. Why wouldn't I have a good time? That's what you were having,—a good time with me,—wasn't it? And say, did you ever stop to think what one day of a working girl's life was like?

GEORGE. One day?

MINNIE. With an alarm clock scaring you out of sweet dreams in the winter, while it's dark, and you get up and dress in the cold and heat a little coffee over a lamp and beat it for the factory,—and stand on your feet all morning, in a noise that would deafen you, feeding a thing you ain't got no interest in? It don't never need no rest! By eleven o'clock you think you're all in, that the morning'll never end, but at noon you get a twenty five cent feed that lasts you until about five in the afternoon,—and then you don't know which way the machine's headed. I've often thought of one of them cutters at Shale's as a sort of monster, watching you all day, waiting to get you when you're too tired to care. (Dreamily.) When it looks all blurred, and you want to put your hand in it.

GEORGE. Good God, Minnie!

MINNIE. And when the whistle blows at night all you have is your little hall bedroom in a rooming house that smells of stale smoke and cabbage. There's no place to go except the streets—but you've just got to go somewhere, to break loose and have a little fun,—even though you're so tired you want to throw yourself on the bed and cry.

(A pause.)

Maybe it's because you're tired. When you're tired that way is when you want a good time most. It's funny, but it's so.

(A pause.)

You ain't got no friends except a few girls with hall bedrooms like yourself, and if a chance comes along for a little excitement, you don't turn it down, I guess.

GEORGE (after a pause). I never knew what your life was like.

MINNIE. Why would you?—with friends, and everything you want, only to buy it? But since the war come on, I tell you, I ain't kicking, I can go to a movie or the theatre once in a while, and buy nice clothes, and I don't get so tired as I used to. I don't want nothing from anybody, I can take care of myself. It's money that makes you free.

GEORGE. Money!

MINNIE. When I looked into this room this morning and saw you standing here in your uniform, I says to myself, "He's changed." Not that you wasn't kind and good natured and generous, George, but you didn't know. How could you? You'd never had a chance to learn anything!

GEORGE (bitterly, yet smiling in spite of himself). That's so!

MINNIE. I remember that first night I ran into you,—I was coming home from your shops, and you made love to me right off the bat! And after that we used to meet by the watering trough on the Lindon road. We were kids then. And it didn't make no difference how tired I was, I'd get over it as soon as I saw you. You were the live wire!

GEORGE. Minnie, tell me, what made you come back to Foxon Falls today?

(He seizes her hand.)

MINNIE (struggling). Don't, George,—don't go and be foolish again!

(The shop whistle blows. She pulls away from him and backs toward

the doorway, upper right.)

There's the noon whistle! Goodbye, I'll be thinking of you, over there.

GEORGE. I'll write to you. Will you write to me, Minnie?

MINNIE (shaking her head). Don't lose any sleep about me. Good luck, George!

(She goes to the doorway, upper right, turns, kisses her hand to

GEORGE and disappears. He goes to the doorway and gazes after her;

presently he raises his hand and waves in answer to another signal,

and smiles. He remains there until MINNIE is out of sight, and then

is about to come back into the room when a man appears on the

sidewalk, seen through the windows. The man is PRAG. He is a gaunt

workman, with high cheek bones and a rather fanatical light in his

blue eyes. He stands motionless, gazing at the house.)

GEORGE (calling). Do you want anything, Prag?

PRAG. I joost come to look at your house, where you live. It is no harm, is it?

GEORGE. None at all.

(PRAG continues to stare at the house, and GEORGE obeys a sudden

impulse.)

Won't you come in, Prag?

PRAG (looking fixedly at the house). No, I stay here.

GEORGE. Come in a while,—don't be unsociable.

(PRAG crosses the lawn and enters, upper right. He surveys the room

curiously, defiantly, and then GEORGE in uniform, as he cones down

the stage.)

You're not working today?

PRAG (with bitter gloom). I lose my job, you don't hear? No, it is nothings to you, and you go away to fight for liberty,—ain't it?

37

GEORGE. How did you lose your job?

PRAG. The foreman come to me last night and says, "Prag I hear you belong to the union. You gets out."

GEORGE (after a moment's hesitation). But—there are plenty of other jobs these days. You can go down to the coast and get more than five dollars a day at a shipyard.

PRAG. It is easy, yes, when you have a little home bought already, and mortgaged, and childrens who go to school here, and a wife a long time sick.

GEORGE. I'm sorry. But weren't you getting along all right here, except your wife's illness? I don't want to be impertinent,—I recognize that it's your affair, but I'd like to know why you joined the union.

PRAG. Why is it you join the army? To fight for somethings you would give your life for—not so? Und you are a soldier,—would you run away from your comrades to live safe and happy? No! That is like me. I lose my job, I go away from my wife and childrens, but it is not for me, it is for all, to get better things for all,—freedoms for all.

GEORGE. Then—you think this isn't a free country.

PRAG. When I sail up the harbour at New York twenty years ago and see that Liberty shining in the sun, I think so, yes. But now I know, for the workmens, she is like the Iron Woman of Nuremberg, with her spikes when she holds you in her arms. You call me a traitor, yes, when I say that.

GEORGE. No—I want to understand.

PRAG. I am born in Bavaria, but I am as good an American as any,—better than you, because I know what I fight for, what I suffer for. I am not afraid of the Junkers here,—I have spirits,—but the Germans at home have no spirits. You think you fight for freedoms, for democracy, but you fight for this! (He waves his hand to indicate the room.) If I had a million dollars, maybe I fight for it, too,—I don't know.

GEORGE. So you think I'm going to fight for this—for money?

PRAG. Are you going to fight for me, for the workmens and their childrens? No, you want to keep your money, to make more of it from your war contracts. It is for the capitalist system you fight.

GEORGE. Come, now, capital has some rights.

PRAG. I know this, that capital is power. What is the workmen's vote against it? against your newspapers and your system? America, she will not be free until your money power is broken. You don't like kings and emperors, no,—you say to us workmens, you are not patriots, you are traitors if you do not work and fight to win this war for democracy against kings. Are we fools that we should worry about kings? Kings will fall of themselves. Now you can put me in jail.

GEORGE. I don't want to put you in jail, God knows! How would you manage it?

PRAG. Why does not the employer say to his workmens, "This is our war, yours and mines. Here is my contract, here is my profits, we will have no secrets, we will work together and talk together and win the war together to make the world brighter for our childrens." Und then we workmens say, "Yes, we will work night and day so hard as we can, because we are free mens."

(A fanatical gleams comes into his eyes.)

But your employer, he don't say that,—no. He says, "This is my contract, this is my shop, and if you join the unions to get your freedoms you cannot work with me, you are traitors!"

(He rises to a frenzy of exaltation.)

After this there will be another war, and the capitalists will be swept away like the kings!

(He pauses; GEORGE is silent.)

Und now I go away, and maybe my wife she die before I get to the shipyard at Newcastle.

(He goes slowly out, upper right, and GEORGE does not attempt to

stay him. Enter ASHER, lower right.)

ASHER. I've just called up the Department in Washington and given them a piece of my mind—told 'em they'd have to conscript labour. Damn these unions, making all this trouble, and especially today, when you're going off. I haven't had a chance to talk to you. Well, you know that I'm proud of you, my boy. Your grandfather went off to the Civil War when he was just about your age.

GEORGE. And he knew what he was going to fight for.

ASHER. What?

GEORGE. I thought I knew, this morning. Now I'm not so sure.

ASHER. You say that, when Germany intended to come over here and crush us, when she got through with the Allies.

GEORGE. No, it's not so simple as that, dad, it's bigger than that.

ASHER. Who's been talking to you? Jonathan Pindar? I wish to God he'd never come to Foxon Falls! I might have known what his opinions would be, with his inheritance. (Reproachfully.) I didn't suppose you could be so easily influenced by sentimentalism, George, I'd hoped you'd got over that.

GEORGE. Are you sure it's sentimentalism, dad? Dr. Jonathan didn't say much, but I'll admit he started me thinking. I've begun to realize a few things—

ASHER. What things?

GEORGE (glancing at the clock on the mantel). I haven't got time to tell you,—I'm afraid I couldn't make it clear, anyway,—it isn't clear in my own mind yet. But,—go slow with this labour business, dad, there's dynamite in it.

ASHER. Dynamite?

GEORGE. Human dynamite. They're full of it,—we're full of it, too, I guess. They're not so different from you and me, though I'll admit that many of them are ignorant, prejudiced and bitter. But this row isn't just the result of restlessness and discontent,—that's the smoke, but the fire's there, too. I've heard enough this morning to be convinced that they're struggling for something fundamental, that has to do with human progress,—the issue behind the war. It's obscured now, in the smoke. Now if that's so you can't ignore it, dad, you can't suppress it, the only thing to do is to sit down with them and try to understand it. If they've got a case, if the union has come to stay, recognize it and deal with it.

ASHER. You—you, my son, are not advising me to recognize the union! To give our employees a voice in our private affairs!

GEORGE (courageously). But is the war our private affair, dad? Hasn't it changed things already?

(ASHER makes a gesture of pain, of repudiation. GEORGE approaches

him appealingly.)

Dad, you know how much we've always been to each other, I'd hate to have any misunderstanding between us,—especially today. I've always accepted your judgment. But I'm over twenty one, I'm going to fight this war, I've got to make up my own mind about it.

ASHER (extending his arms and putting his hands on GEORGE'S shoulders). Something's upset you today, my boy,—you don't know what you're saying. When you get over there and take command of your men you'll see things in a truer proportion.

GEORGE. No, I can't leave it this way, dad. I've come to feel this thing, it's got hold of me now, I shan't change. And I'll be thinking of it over there, all the time, if we don't talk it out.

ASHER. For God's sake, George, don't speak of it again,—don't think of it! There's no sacrifice I wouldn't make for you, in reason, but you're asking me to go against my life-long convictions. As your father, I forbid you to entertain such ideas—(he breaks off, choking). Don't speak of them, don't think of them!

(TIMOTHY FARRELL Steps inside the doorway, upper right, followed by

BERT, and after a few moments by DR. JONATHAN.)

TIMOTHY. Excuse me sir, but you asked me to be letting you know if I heard anything. There's a meeting called for tonight, and they'll strike on Monday morning. It's certain I am, from the way the men are talking,—unless ye'd agree to meet the committee this afternoon and come to an understanding like.

ASHER. Let them strike. If they burned down the shops this afternoon, I wouldn't stop them! (He waves TIMOTHY Off.) My boy is leaving for France, and I'm going to New York with him.

TIMOTHY (with a sudden flaring up of sympathy). It's meself has a boy going, too, Mr. Pindar. And maybe it's almost the last I'll be seeing of him, this noon hour. Just a word with ye, before it's too late, sir.

ASHER (suppressing him). No, let them strike!

(He turns to hide his emotion and then rushes out of the door, lower

right. GEORGE and BERT come forward and stand with TIMOTHY, silent

after ASHER's dramatic exit; when TIMOTHY perceives DR. JONATHAN.)

TIMOTHY. Did you see my Minnie, doctor? She went to your house.

DR. JONATHAN. I met her on the street just now, and left her with Mrs. Prag.

GEORGE. Prag's wife! You've been to see her?

DR. JONATHAN. Yes. Her condition is serious. She needs a nurse, and Minnie volunteered.

TIMOTHY. My Minnie, is it? Then she won't be going back to Newcastle.

DR. JONATHAN (looking at GEORGE). She won't be going back to Newcastle.

TIMOTHY. That's Minnie! (he turns to GEORGE). Well, goodbye, Mr. George,—I'll say God bless you again. (He looks at BERT.) You'll be fighting over there, the pair of you, for freedom. Have an eye on him, Sir, if you can,—give him some good advice.

GEORGE (his hand on BERT'S shoulder). Bert can take care of himself, I guess. I'll be needing the advice!

(He shakes hands with TIMOTHY.)

CURTAIN.

ACT II

SCENE: A fairly large room in DR. JONATHAN's house in Foxon Falls, which

  has been converted into a laboratory. The house antedates the

  PINDAR mansion, having been built in the first decade of the

  nineteenth century, and though not large, has a certain distinction

  and charm. The room has a panelled wainscoting and a carved wooden

  mantel, middle left, painted white, like the doors. Into the

  fireplace is set a Franklin stove. The windows at the rear have

  small panes; the lower sashes are raised; the tops of the hollyhocks

  and foxgloves in the garden bed may be seen above the window sills,

  and the apple trees beyond. Under the windows is a long table, on

  which are chemical apparatus. A white enamelled sink is in the rear

  right corner. The walls are whitewashed, the wooden floor bare. A

  door, left, in the rear, leads into DR. JONATHAN'S office; another,

  middle right, into a little front hall.

TIME: A July morning, 1918.

  MINNIE FARRELL, in the white costume worn by nurses and laboratory

  workers, is at the bench, pouring liquid into a test tube and

  holding its up to the light, when DR. JONATHAN enters from the

  right.

DR. JONATHAN. Has anyone been in, Minnie?

MINNIE (turning, with the test tube in her hand). Now, what a question to ask, Dr. Jonathan! Was there ever a morning or afternoon that somebody didn't stray in here with their troubles? (Fiercely.) They don't think a scientist has a real job,—they don't understand, if you put this across—(she holds up the test tube)—you'll save the lives of thousands of soldiers, and a few ordinary folks, too, I guess. But you won't let me tell anyone.

DR. JONATHAN. It will be time enough to tell them when we do put it across.

MINNIE. But we're going to,—that is, you're going to.

DR. JONATHAN. You're too modest, Minnie.

MINNIE. Me modest! But what makes me sore is that they don't give you a chance to put this thing across. Dr. Senn's a back number, and if they're sick they come here and expect you to cure 'em for nothing.

DR. JONATHAN. But they can't complain if I don't cure them.

MINNIE. And half the time they ain't sick at all,—they only imagine it.

DR. JONATHAN. Well, that's interesting too,—part of a doctor's business. It's pretty hard to tell in these days where the body ends and the soul begins.

MINNIE. It looks like you're cutting out the minister, too. You'd ought to be getting his salary.

DR. JONATHAN. Then I'd have to do his job.

MINNIE. I get you—you'd be paid to give 'em all the same brand of dope. You wouldn't be free.

DR. JONATHAN. To experiment.

MINNIE. You couldn't be a scientist. Say, every time I meet the minister I want to cry, he says to himself, "She ran away from Jesus and went to the bad. What right has she got to be happy?" And Mrs. Pindar's just the same. If you leave the straight and narrow path you can't never get back—they keep pushing you off.

DR. JONATHAN (who has started to work at the bench). I've always had my doubts about your sins, Minnie.

45

MINNIE. Oh, I was a sinner, all right, they'll never get that out of their craniums. But being a sinner isn't a patch on being a scientist! It's nearly a year now since you took me in. The time's flown! When I was in the Pindar Shops, and in the Wire Works at Newcastle I could always beat the other girls to the Main Street when the whistle blew, but now I'm sorry when night comes. I can't hardly wait to get back here—honest to God! Say, Dr. Jonathan, I've found out one thing,—it's being in the right place that keeps a man or a woman straight. If you're in the wrong place, all the religion in the world won't help you. If you're doing work you like, that you've got an interest in, and that's some use, you don't need religion (she pauses). Why, that's religion,—it ain't preaching and praying and reciting creeds, it's doing—it's fun. There's no reason why religion oughtn't to be fun, is there?

DR. JONATHAN. None at all!

MINNIE. Now, if we could get everybody in the right job, we wouldn't have any more wars, I guess.

DR. JONATHAN. The millennium always keeps a lap ahead—we never catch up with it.

MINNIE. Well, I don't want to catch up with it. We wouldn't have anything more to do. Say, it's nearly eleven o'clock—would you believe it?—and I've been expecting Mr. Pindar to walk in here with the newspaper. I forgot he was in Washington.

DR. JONATHAN. He was expected home this morning.

MINNIE. What gets me is the way he hangs around here, too, like everybody else, and yet I've heard him call you a Socialist, and swear he hasn't any use for Socialists.

DR. JONATHAN. Perhaps he's trying to find out what a Socialist is. Nobody seems to know.

MINNIE. He don't know, anyway. If it hadn't been for you, his shops would have been closed down last winter.

DR. JONATHAN. It looks as if they'd be closed down now, anyway.

MINNIE (concerned, looking up). Is that so? Well, he won't recognize the union—he doesn't know what century he's living in. But he's human, all the same, and he's good to the people he's fond of, like my father,—and he sure loves George. He's got

George's letters all wore out, reading them, to people. (A pause.) He don't know where George is, does he, Dr. Jonathan?

DR. JONATHAN. Somewhere in France.

MINNIE. We spotted Bert because he's with the Marines, at that place where they put a crimp in the Huns the other day when they were going to walk into Paris.

DR. JONATHAN. Chateau-Thierry.

MINNIE. I'll leave it to you. But say, Dr. Jonathan, things don't look good to me,—I'm scared we won't get enough of our boys over there before the deal's closed up. I've got so I don't want to look at a paper.

(A brief silence.)

I never told you George wrote me a couple of letters, did I?

DR. JONATHAN. No, I'm quite sure you didn't.

MINNIE. I never told nobody. His father and mother would be wild if they knew it. I didn't answer them—I just sent him two post cards with no writing on except the address—just pictures.

DR. JONATHAN. Pictures?

MINNIE. One of the Pindar Church and the Other of the Pindar Shops. I guess he'll understand they were from me, all right. You see, when I ran away from the Pindar Shops and the Pindar Church—I always connect them together—I was stuck on George. That's why I ran away.

DR. JONATHAN. I see.

MINNIE. Oh, I never let him know. I don't know why I told you—I had to tell somebody,—and you won't give me away.

DR. JONATHAN. You may count on me.

MINNIE. He didn't care nothing about me, really. But you can't help liking George. He's human, all right! If he was boss of the Pindar Shops there wouldn't be any strike.

(A knock at the door, right.)

I wonder who's butting in now!

(She goes to the door and jerks it open.)

(A man's voice, without.) Good morning, Miss Farrell. Is the doctor in?

MINNIE. This is his busy day.

DR. JONATHAN (going toward the door). Oh, it's you, Hillman. Come in.

MINNIE. I guess I'll go for the mail.

(With a resigned expression she goes oust right as HILLMAN comes in, followed by RENCH and FERSEN. They are the strike committee. HILLMAN is a little man, with red hair and a stiff, bristling red moustache. He holds himself erect, and walks on the balls of his feet, quietly. RENCH is tall and thin, with a black moustache, like a seal's. He has a loud, nasal voice, and an assertive manner. FERSEN is a blond Swede.)

(DR. JONATHAN puts one or two objects in place on the bench. His manner is casual but cordial, despite the portentous air of the Committee.)

(The men, their hats in their hands, go toward the bench and inspect

the test tubes and apparatus.)

RENCH (New England twang). Always manage to have something on hand when you ain't busy with the folks, doctor. It must be interestin' to fool with these here chemicals.

DR. JONATHAN. It keeps me out of mischief.

HILLMAN. I guess you haven't much time to get into mischief.

FERSEN. We don't like to bother you.

DR. JONATHAN. No bother, Fersen,—sit down. (He draws forward some chairs, and they sit down.) How is the baby?

FERSEN. Oh, she is fine, now, since we keep her outside in the baby carriage, like you tell us.

(FERSEN grins, and immediately becomes serious again. A brief

silence.)

HILLMAN (clearing his throat). The fact is, Dr. Jonathan, the boys have struck,—voted last night to walk out at noon today.

FERSEN. We thought we tell you now. You been such a good friend to us and our families.

DR. JONATHAN. But isn't this rather sudden, with Mr. Pindar in Washington?

RENCH. We couldn't wait no longer,—he's been standing us off for more than a year. When he comes back from Washington there'll be nothing doing. He's got to recognize the union or lose his contract.

DR. JONATHAN. He may prefer to lose his contract.

RENCH. Well, he can afford to. Then he can go to hell.

HILLMAN. Hold on, Sam, that ain't no way to talk to the doctor!

RENCH. I didn't mean no disrespect to him. He don't go 'round preachin', like some fellers I could mention, but actions is louder than words. Ain't that the reason we're here, because he sympathizes with us and thinks we're entitled to a little more of this freedom that's bein' handed 'round? We want you to help us, doctor.

DR. JONATHAN. It seems to me you've come a little late, Rench,—after the event.

HILLMAN. Maybe if you'd said a word, they'd never have voted to strike.

FERSEN. But you never said nothing, Doctor.

DR. JONATHAN. Well, when you get around to admitting doctors to your labour unions, perhaps they'll talk.

HILLMAN. If all the doctors was like you!

DR. JONATHAN. Give 'em a chance, Hillman.

HILLMAN. We don't have to explain to you why we want the union,—it's the only way we'll ever get a say about the conditions in which we work and live, now that the day of individual bargaining is gone by. You understand. Mr. Pindar raised our wages when we threatened to strike last fall, but he calculates to drop 'em again when the soldiers come home.

FERSEN (nodding). Sure thing!

HILLMAN. It's this way, doctor. We notice Mr. Pindar comin' in here to see you every day or so,—like the rest of Foxon Falls. And we thought you could make him see this thing straight, if any man could.

DR. JONATHAN. So the shops will be idle.

RENCH. Not a shaft'll turn over till he recognizes the union.

HILLMAN. We don't want to do nothin' to obstruct the war, but we've got to have our rights.

DR. JONATHAN. Can you get your rights now, without obstructing the war?

RENCH (aggressively). I get what you're driving at, doctor. You're going to say that we've just reached quantity production on these here machines, and if labour gets from under now, the Huns win. But tell me this,—where'll labour be if America wins and our Junkers (he pronounces the J) come out on top?—as they callate to.

DR. JONATHAN (smiling). When a building with dry rot catches fire, Rench, can you put limit to how much of it will burn?

RENCH (after a pause). Maybe not. I get you—but—

DR. JONATHAN. No nation, no set of men in any nation can quench that fire or make the world that is coming out of this war. They may think they can, but they can't.

HILLMAN. That's so!

DR. JONATHAN. Germany will be beaten, because it is the temper of the nation, the temper of the times—your temper. You don't want Germany to win, Rench?

RENCH. No, I guess not.

DR. JONATHAN. And if you don't work here, you'll go off to work somewhere else.

RENCH. Where they recognize the union.

DR. JONATHAN. A good many of your friends have enlisted, haven't they? (RENCH nods.) And what do you suppose they are fighting for?

RENCH. For the same thing as we want, a square deal.

DR. JONATHAN. And what do you think George Pindar is fighting for?

RENCH. I ain't got nothing to say against him.

DR. JONATHAN. If you close down the Pindar Shops, won't it mean that a few more of your friends will lose their lives? These men are fighting for something they don't yet understand, but when they come back they'll know more about it. Why not wait until George Pindar comes back?

RENCH. He mayn't never come back.

DR. JONATHAN. Give him the opportunity.

RENCH. I like George,—he's always been friendly—what we call a common man up here in New England—naturally democratic. But at bottom employers is all alike. What makes you think he won't take his ideas about labour from the old man?

DR. JONATHAN. Because he belongs to the generation that fights this war.

HILLMAN (shuffling). It ain't no use, doctor. Unless you can bring Mr. Pindar 'round, the shops'll close down.

DR. JONATHAN. I can't, but something else can.

HILLMAN. What?

DR. JONATHAN. Circumstances. No man can swim up stream very long in these days, Hillman. Wait a while, and see.

RENCH (rising). We've voted to put this strike through, and by God, we'll do it.

FERSEN (rising and shaking hands with DR. JONATHAN). It's fine weather, doctor.

RENCH (bursting into a laugh). He's like the man who said, when Congress declared war, "It's a fine day for it!" It's a fine day for a strike!

HILLMAN (who has risen, shaking hands with DR. JONATHAN). But you'll talk to Mr. Pindar, anyway?

DR. JONATHAN (smiling). Yes, I'll talk with him.

(Enter TIMOTHY FARRELL, right, in working clothes.)

TIMOTHY. Good morning, doctor. (Surveying the committee.) So it's here ye are, after voting to walk out of the shops just when we're beginning to turn out the machines for the soldiers!

RENCH. If we'd done right we'd have called the strike a year ago.

TIMOTHY. Fine patriots ye are—as I'm sure the doctor is after telling you—to let the boys that's gone over there be murdered because ye must have your union!

HILLMAN. If Mr. Pindar recognizes the union, Timothy, we'll go to work tomorrow.

TIMOTHY. He recognize the union! He'll recognize the devil first! Even Dr. Jonathan, with all the persuasion he has, couldn't get Mr. Pindar to recognize the union. He'll close down the shops, and it's hunting a job I'll be, and I here going on thirty years.

RENCH. If he closes the shops—what then? The blood of the soldiers'll be on his head, not ours. If there were fewer scabs in the country—

HILLMAN. Hold on, Sam.

TIMOTHY. A scab, is it? If I was the government do you know what I'd do with the likes of you—striking in war time? I'd send ye over there to fight the Huns with your bare fists. I'm a workman meself, but I don't hold with traitors.

RENCH. Who's a traitor? It's you who are a traitor to your class. If a union card makes a man a traitor, your own son had one in his pocket the day he enlisted.

TIMOTHY. A traitor, and he fighting for his country, while you'd be skulking here to make trouble for it!

(MINNIE appears on the threshold of the door, right. DR. JONATHAN,

who is the first to perceive from her expression that there is

something wrong, takes a step toward her. After a moment's silence

she comes up to TIMOTHY and lays a hand on his arm.)

TIMOTHY (bewildered). What is it, Minnie?

MINNIE. Come home, father.

TIMOTHY. What is it? It's not a message ye have—it's not a message about Bert?

(MINNIE continues to gaze at him.)

The one I'd be looking for these many days! (He seizes her.) Can't ye speak, girl? Is the boy dead?

53

MINNIE. Yes, father.

TIMOTHY (puts his hand to his forehead and lets fall his hat. DR. JONATHAN picks it up). Me boy! The dirty devils have killed him!

MINNIE. Come, father, we'll go home.

TIMOTHY. Home, is it? It's back to the shops I'm going. (To the committee) Damn ye—we'll run the shops in spite of ye! Where's me hat?

(DR. JONATHAN hands it to him as the committee file out in silence.)

Come with me as far as the shops, Minnie. Thank you, doctor—(as DR. JONATHAN gives him the hat)—it's you I'll be wanting to see when I get me mind again.

(DR. JONATHAN goes with TIMOTHY and MINNIE as far as the door,

right, and then comes back thoughtfully to the bench, takes up a

test tube and holds it to the light. Presently ASHER PINDAR

appears in the doorway, right.)

ASHER. Good morning, Jonathan.

DR. JONATHAN. Good morning, Asher. I didn't know you'd got back from Washington.

ASHER. I came in on the mail train.

DR. JONATHAN. Have you been to the office?

ASHER. No. I stopped at the house to speak to Augusta, and then—(he speaks a trifle apologetically)—well, I went for a little walk.

DR. JONATHAN. A walk.

ASHER. I've been turning something over in my mind. And the country looked so fine and fresh I crossed the covered bridge to the other side of the river. When George was a child I used to go over there with him on summer afternoons. He was such a companionable little shaver—he'd drop his toys when he'd see me coming home from the office. I can see him now, running along that road over there, stopping to pick funny little bouquets—the kind a child makes, you know—ox-eyed daisies and red clover and buttercups all mixed up together, and he'd carry them home and put them in a glass on the desk in my study.

(A pause.)

It seems like yesterday! It's hard to realize that he's a grown man, fighting over there in the trenches, and that any moment I may get a telegram, or be called to the telephone—Have you seen today's paper?

DR. JONATHAN. No.

ASHER. It looks like more bad news,—the Germans have started another one of those offensives. I was afraid they were getting ready for it. West of Verdun this time. And George may be in that sector, for all I know. How is this thing going to end, Jonathan? That damned military machine of theirs seems invincible—it keeps grinding on. Are we going to be able to stem the tide, or to help stem it with a lot of raw youths. They've only had a year's training.

DR. JONATHAN. Germany can't win, Asher.

ASHER. What makes you say that? We started several years too late.

Dr. JONATHAN. And Germany started several centuries too late.

ASHER. My God, I hope you're right. I don't know.

(He walks once or twice up and down the room..)

I've had another letter.

DR. JONATHAN. This morning?

ASHER. No—I got it before I left for Washington. But I didn't bring it in to you I wanted to think about it.

(He draws the letter, together with a folded paper, from his pocket,

and lays the paper down on the bench. Then he adjusts his glasses and begins to read.)

"Dear dad,

"The sky is the colour of smeared charcoal. We haven't been in the trenches long enough to evolve web feet, so mine are resting on a duck board spread over a quagmire of pea soup. The Heinies are right here, soaking in another ditch beyond a barbed wire fence, about the distance of second base from the home plate. Such is modern war!

"But these aren't the things that trouble me. Last night, when I was wet to the skin and listening to the shells—each singing its own song in the darkness—I was able to think with astonishing ease better than if I were sitting at a mahogany desk in a sound proof room! I was thinking over the talk we had the day I left home,—do you remember it?—about the real issue of this war. I've thought of it time and again, but I've never written you about it. Since I have been in France I have had a liberal education gathered from all sorts and conditions of men. Right here in the trench near me are a street car conductor, a haberdasher, a Swedish farm hand, a grocery clerk, a college professor, a Pole from the Chicago Stock Yards, an Irish American janitor of a New York apartment house, and Grierson from Cleveland, whose father has an income of something like a million a year. We have all decided that this is a war for the under dog, whether he comes from Belgium or Armenia or that so-called land of Democracy, the United States of America. The hope that spurs us on and makes us willing to endure these swinish surroundings and die here in the mud, if need be, is that the world will now be reorganized on some intelligent basis; that Grierson and I, if we get back, won't have to rot on a large income and petrified ideas, but will have some interesting and creative work to do. Economic inequalities must be reduced, and those who toil must be given a chance to live, not merely to exist. Their lives must include a little leisure, comfortable homes, art and beauty and above all an education that none of us, especially those of us who went to universities, never got,—but which now should be available for all.

"The issue of this war is industrial democracy, without which political democracy is a farce. That sentence is Dr. Jonathan's. But when I was learning how to use the bayonet from a British sergeant in Picardy I met an English manufacturer from Northumberland. He is temporarily an officer. I know your opinion of theorists, but this man is working out the experiment with human chemicals. After all, the Constitution of the United States, now antiquated and revered, once existed only in the brains of French theorists! In the beginning was the Word, but the deed must follow. This Englishman, whose name is Wray, has given me the little pamphlet he wrote from his experience, and I shall send it to you.

"Though I am writing this letter in what to me is a solemn and undoubtedly exalted hour, I am sure that my mind was never clearer or saner. Dad, I have set my heart on inaugurating an experiment in industrial democracy in Foxon Falls! I'd like to be able to think—if anything happened to me—that the Pindar shops were among the first in America to recognize that we are living in a new era and a changed world."

(ASHER walks over to the bench and lays down the open letter on it.)

If anything should happen to that boy, Jonathan, there wouldn't be anything in life left for me! Industrial democracy! So you put that into his head! Socialism, I suppose.

DR. JONATHAN. No, experimental science.

ASHER. Call it what you like. What surprises me is, when I look back over the months you've been here, how well we've got along in spite of your views.

DR. JONATHAN. Why not say in spite of yours, Asher?

ASHER (smiling involuntarily). Well, it's been a comfort to drop in here and talk to you, in spite of what you believe. You've got the gift of sympathy, Jonathan. But I don't approve of you're spending your time in this sort of work—(he waves a hand toward the bench)—which may never come to anything, and in doctoring people for nothing and patching up their troubles. I daresay you enjoy it, but what worries me is how you are going to live?

DR. JONATHAN. By practising your cardinal virtue, thrift.

ASHER. I've got a proposal to make to you part of a scheme I've been turning over in my mind for the last six months—and when George's letter came I decided to put it through. I went to New York and had Sterry, a corporation lawyer, draw it up. I'm going to prove I'm not a mossback. It will reorganize the Pindar Shops.

DR. JONATHAN. Well, that's good news.

ASHER. First, with reference to your part in it, I shall establish a free hospital for my employees, and put you in charge of it, at a salary of five thousand a year. After all, you're the only Pindar left except George, and I'm satisfied that as a doctor you're up to the job, since you've driven Dr. Senn out of business.

DR. JONATHAN. Practical proof, Asher. Fortunately Dr. Senn has enough to live on.

ASHER. In offering you this position I have only one stipulation to make—(he clears his throat)—it's about Minnie Farrell. I think the world of Timothy, I wouldn't willingly hurt his feelings, but I can't have Minnie with you in the hospital, Jonathan. You deserve a great deal of credit for what you've done for the girl, you've kept her out of mischief, but considering her past, her life at Newcastle—well, even if I approved of having her in the hospital Augusta would never hear of it. And then she had some sort of an affair with George—I daresay there was nothing wrong—

DR. JONATHAN. Wrong is a question of code, Asher. We've all had pasts—What interests me is Minnie's future.

ASHER. Of course you wouldn't decline my offer on Minnie's account.

DR. JONATHAN. On my own account, Asher. We'll say no more about Minnie.

ASHER. You refuse to help me, when I'm starting out on a liberal scheme which I thought you would be the first to endorse?

DR. JONATHAN. I have not refused to help you,—but you have not told me the scheme?

ASHER. Well. (He' taps the paper in his hand.) For those employees who serve me faithfully I have arranged pensions.

DR. JONATHAN. For those, in other words, who refrain from taking their destinies in their own hands, and who do as you wish.

ASHER. For those who are industrious and make no trouble. And I have met the objection that they have no share in the enterprise by allowing them, on favourable terms, to acquire stock in the company.

DR. JONATHAN. I see. You will let them acquire half of the stock, in order that they may have an equal voice.

ASHER. Equal? It's my company, isn't it?

DR. JONATHAN. At present.

ASHER. I supply the capital. Furthermore, I have arranged for a system of workmen's committees, which I recognize, and with which I will continually consult. That's democratic enough—isn't it? If the men have any grievances, these will be presented in an orderly manner through the committees.

DR. JONATHAN. And if you find the demands—reasonable, you grant them.

ASHER. Certainly. But one thing I set my face against as a matter of principle, I won't recognize the unions.

DR. JONATHAN. But—who is to enforce the men's side of this contract?

ASHER. What do you mean?

DR. JONATHAN. What guarantee have they, other than a union organization, that you will keep faith?

ASHER. My word.

DR. JONATHAN. Oh!

ASHER. Never in my life have I regarded my possessions as my own. I am a trustee.

DR. JONATHAN. The sole trustee.

ASHER. Under God.

DR. JONATHAN. And you have God's proxy. Well, it seems to me that that is a very delightful arrangement, Asher—William appears to approve of it, too.

ASHER. William? William who?

DR. JONATHAN. William Hohenzollern.

ASHER. You compare me to the Kaiser!

DR. JONATHAN. Only in so far as you have in common a certain benevolence, Asher. Wouldn't your little plan, if your workmen accepted it, keep you in as a benevolent autocrat?

ASHER. Me? an autocrat?

DR. JONATHAN. You are preparing to give your men more privileges, and perhaps more money on the condition that they will renounce rights to which they are entitled as free men. You are ready to grant anything but a constitution. So is William.

ASHER. Do you seriously suggest that I give labour a voice in my business?

DR. JONATHAN. Doesn't George suggest it, when he pleads for industrial democracy? He seems to think that he is ready to give his life for it. And Bert Farrell has already given his life for it.

ASHER (agitatedly). What? Timothy's boy, Bert? Is he dead? Why didn't you tell me?

DR. JONATHAN (gently). I've had no chance. Minnie and Timothy were here just before you came in.

ASHER. Oh God, I'm sorry—I'm sorry for Timothy. It might have been—I'll go and see Timothy. Where is he?—at his house.

DR. JONATHAN. No, at the shops. He wanted to keep working until they close down.

ASHER (who has started for the door, right, turns). What do you mean?

(There is a knock at the door.)

DR. JONATHAN. I mean that the moment has come, Asher, to remember George. That your opportunity is here—heed it.

ASHER. I can't, I won't desert my principles

(The knock is repeated. DR. JONATHAN goes to the door and opens it.

Enter, in the order named, HILLMAN, RENCH and FERSEN.)

HILLMAN. Beg your pardon, Mr. Pindar, we've been waiting for you at the office, and we heard you was here.

ASHER (facing them with a defiance almost leonine). Well, what is it?

HILLMAN (glancing at DR. JONATHAN). There's a matter we'd like to talk over with you, Mr. Pindar, as soon as convenient.

ASHER. This is as convenient as any time, right now.

HILLMAN. The men voted to strike, last night. Maybe Dr. Jonathan has told you.

ASHER. Voted to strike behind my back while I was in Washington attending to the nation's business!

RENCH. It ain't as if this was anything new, Mr. Pindar, as if we hadn't been discussing this here difference for near a year. You've had your warning right along.

ASHER. Didn't I raise your wages last January?

HILLMAN. Wait a minute, Mr. Pindar. (He looks at DR. JONATHAN.) It oughtn't to be only what you say—what capital says. Collective bargaining is only right and fair, now that individual bargaining has gone by. We want to be able to talk to you as man to man,—that's only self-respecting on our part. All you've got to do is to say one word, that you'll recognize the union, and I'll guarantee there won't be any trouble.

RENCH. If you don't, we walk out at noon.

HILLMAN (with an attempt at conciliation). I know if we could sit down and talk this thing out with you, Mr. Pindar, you'd see it reasonable.

ASHER. Reasonable? Treasonable, you mean,—to strike when the lives of hundreds of thousands of your fellow countrymen depend on your labour.

RENCH. We ain't striking—you're striking!

FERSEN (nodding). That's right!

RENCH. We're ready to go back to work this afternoon if you treat us like Americans. (FERSEN nods.) You say we're obstructing the war by not giving in,— what's the matter with you giving in? Ain't the employers just as much traitors as we?

HILLMAN. Hold on, Sam,—we won't get nowhere by calling names. Let's discuss it cool!

ASHER. I refuse to discuss it.

(He takes the paper out of his docket and holds it up.)

Do you see this paper? It's a plan I had made, of my own free will, for the betterment and advancement of the working class. It was inspired by the suggestion of my son, who is now fighting in France. I came back to Foxon Falls this morning happy in the hope that I was to do something to encourage what was good in labour—and how have I been met? With a demand, with a threat. I was a fool to think you could stand decent treatment!

(He seizes the paper, and tears it in two.)

HILLMAN. Wait a minute, Mr. Pindar. If you won't listen to us, maybe Dr. Jonathan would say a word for us. He understands how we feel.

ASHER (savagely tearing the paper in two, and then again in four). That's my answer! I won't have Dr. Pindar or anyone else interfering in my private affairs.

RENCH. All right—I guess we're wasting time here, boys. We walk out and stay out. (Threateningly.) Not a shaft'll turn over in them shops until you recognize the union. And if that's treason, go back to Washington and tell 'em so. Come on boys!

(He walks out, followed by FERSEN, nodding, and lastly by HILLMAN,

who glances at DR. JONATHAN. ASHER stares hard at them as they

leave. Then an expression of something like agony crosses his

face.)

ASHER. My God, it's come! My shops shut down, for the first time in my life, and when the government relies on me!

(DR. JONATHAN stoops down and picks up the fragments of the document

from the floor.)

What are you doing?

DR. JONATHAN. Trying to save the pieces, Asher.

ASHER. I've got no use for them now.

DR. JONATHAN. But history may have.

ASHER. History. History will brand these men with shame for all time. I'll fix 'em! I'll go back to Washington, and if the government has any backbone, if it's still American, they'll go to work or fight! (Pointedly.) This is what comes of your Utopian dreams, of your socialism!

(A POLAK WOMAN is seen standing in the doorway, right.)

WOMAN. Doctor!

DR. JONATHAN. Yes.

WOMAN. My baby is seek—I think maybe you come and see him. Mrs. Ladislaw she tell me you cure her little boy, and that maybe you come, if I ask you.

DR. JONATHAN. Yes, I'll come. What is your name?

WOMAN. Sasenoshky.

DR. JONATHAN. Your husband is in the shops?

WOMAN. He was, doctor. Now he is in the American army.

DR. JONATHAN. Sasenoshky—in the American army.

WOMAN (proudly). Yes, he is good American now,—he fight to make them free in the old country, too.

DR. JONATHAN. Well, we'll have a look at the baby. He may be in the White House some day—President Sasenoshky! I'll be back, Asher.

(The noon whistle blows.)

ASHER. That's the signal! I'll get along, too.

DR. JONATHAN. Where are you going?

ASHER. I guess it doesn't make much difference where I go.

63

(He walks out, followed by DR. JONATHAN and the WOMAN. The room is empty for a moment, and then MINNIE FARRELL enters through the opposite door, left, from DR. JONATHAN'S office. She gazes around the room, and then goes resolutely to the bench and takes up several test tubes in turn, holding theme to the light. Suddenly her eye falls on GEORGE'S letter, which ASHER has left open on the bench with the envelope beside it. MINNIE Slowly reaches out and picks it up, and then holds it to her lips... She still has the letter in her hand, gazing at it, when AUGUSTA PINDAR enters, right.)

AUGUSTA. Oh, I thought Mr. Pindar was here!

MINNIE. Perhaps he's been here—I don't know. I just came in. (She hesitates a second, then goes to the bench and lays the letter down.)

AUGUSTA. He must have been here,—he told me he was coming to talk with Dr. Pindar.

(She approaches the bench and glances at the letter.)

Isn't that a letter from my son?

MINNIE (a little defiantly, yet almost in tears). I guess it is.

AUGUSTA. It was written to you?

MINNIE. No.

AUGUSTA. Then what were you doing with it?

MINNIE. I just—picked it up. You think I was reading it? Well, I wouldn't.

AUGUSTA. Then how did you know it was written by my son?

64

(MINNIE is silent.)

You must be familiar with his handwriting. I think I'd better take it. (She folds it up and puts it in the envelope.) Does George write to you?

MINNIE. I've had letters from him.

AUGUSTA. Since he went to France?

MINNIE. Yes.

AUGUSTA (after a pause). I've never approved of Dr. Findar employing you here. I warned him against you—I told him that you would betray his kindness as you betrayed mine, but he wouldn't listen to me. I told him that a girl who was capable of drawing my son into an intrigue while she was a member of the church and of my Bible class, a girl who had the career you had in Newcastle, couldn't become a decent and trustworthy woman. The very fact that you had the audacity to come back to Foxon Falls and impose on Dr. Pindar's simplicity, proves it.

MINNIE. You know all about me, Mrs. Pindar.

AUGUSTA. I wasn't born yesterday.

MINNIE. Oh, ladies like you, Christian ladies, are hard! They won't believe nothing good of anybody—only the bad. You've always been sheltered, you've always had everything you'd want, and you come and judge us working girls. You'd drive me out of the only real happiness I ever had, being here with a man like Dr. Jonathan, doing work it's a pleasure to do—a pleasure every minute!—work that may do good to thousands of people, to the soldiers over there—maybe to George, for all you know! (She burst into tears.) You can't understand—how could you? After all, you're his mother. I oughtn't to forget it.

AUGUSTA. Yes, I'm his mother. And you? You haven't given up the idea that he may marry you some day, if you stay here and pretend to have reformed. You write to him. George may have been foolish, but he isn't as foolish as that!

MINNIE. He doesn't care about me.

AUGUSTA. I'm glad you realize it. But you mean to stay here in Foxon Falls, nevertheless. You take advantage of Dr. Pindar, who is easily imposed upon, as his father was before him. But if I told you that you might harm Dr. Pindar by staying here, interfere with his career, would you be willing to leave?

MINNIE. Me? Me doing Dr. Jonathan harm?

AUGUSTA, Yes. I happen to know that he has very little money. He makes none, he never asks anyone for a bill. He spends what he has on this kind of thing—research, for the benefit of humanity, as he thinks,—but very little research work succeeds, and even then it doesn't pay.

MINNIE. He doesn't care about money.

AUGUSTA. Perhaps not. He is one of those impractical persons who have to be looked out for, if they are fortunate enough to have anyone to look out for them. Since he is a cousin of my husband, Mr. Pindar considers him as one of his many responsibilities. Mr. Pindar has always had, in a practical way, the welfare of his working people at heart, and now he proposes to establish a free hospital for them and to put Dr. Pindar in charge of it. This will give him a good living as well as a definite standing in the community, which he needs also.

MINNIE. He's the biggest man in Foxon Falls today!

AUGUSTA. That is as one thinks. At any rate, he has this opportunity. Are you going to stand in the way of it?

MINNIE. Me stand in the way of it?

AUGUSTA. If Dr. Pindar accepts the place, you can't go with him,—you will have to find some other position. Mr. Pindar is firm about that, and rightly so. But I believe Dr. Pindar would be quite capable of refusing rather than inconvenience anyone with whom he is connected.

MINNIE. You're right there!

AUGUSTA. He's quixotic.

MINNIE. If that's a compliment, you're right again.

AUGUSTA. It isn't exactly a compliment.

MINNIE. I guess you mean he's queer—but you're wrong—you're wrong! He's the only man in Foxon Falls who knows what kind of a world we're going to live in from now on. Why? Because he's a scientist, because he's trained himself to think straight, because he understands people like you and people like me. He don't blame us for what we do—he knows why we do it.

(A pause.)

That's the reason I try not to blame you for being hard—you can't understand a girl like me. You can't understand George.

AUGUSTA (white). We'll leave my son out of the conversation, if you please. We were talking of Dr. Pindar. You seem to have some consideration for him, at least.

MINNIE. I'd go to the electric chair for him!

AUGUSTA. I'm not asking you to do that.

MINNIE. You want me to go away and get another place. I remember a lesson you gave us one day in Bible class, "Judge not, that you be not judged,"—that was what you talked about. But you're judging me on what you think is my record,—and you'd warn people against hiring me. If everybody was a Christian like that these days, I'd starve or go on the street.

AUGUSTA. We have to pay for what we do.

MINNIE. And you make it your business to see that we pay.

(A pause.)

Well, I'll go. I didn't know how poor Dr. Jonathan was,—he never said anything about it to me. I'll disappear.

AUGUSTA. You have some good in you.

MINNIE. Don't begin talking to me about good!

(TIMOTHY FARRELL enters, right.)

TIMOTHY. Good morning, ma'am. (Looking at MINNIE and AUGUSTA). I came to fetch Minnie to pass an hour with me.

AUGUSTA (agitated and taken aback). Were—were having a little talk. (She goes up to TIMOTHY.) I'm distressed to hear about Bert!

TIMOTHY. Thank you for your sympathy, ma'am.

(A brief silence. Enter ASHER, right.)

ASHER (surveying the group). You here, Augusta? (He goes up to TIMOTHY and presses his hand.) I wanted to see you, Timothy,—I understand how you feel. We both gave our sons in this war. You've lost yours, and I expect to lose mine.

AUGUSTA. Asher!

TIMOTHY. Don't say that, Mr. Pindar

ASHER. Why not? What right have I to believe, after what has happened in my shops today, that he'll come back?

TIMOTHY. God forbid that he should be lost, too! There's trouble enough—sorrow enough—

ASHER. Sorrow enough! But if a man has one friend left, Timothy, it's something.

TIMOTHY (surprised). Sure, I hope it's a friend I am, sir,—a friend this thirty years.

ASHER. We're both old fashioned, Timothy,—we can't help that.

TIMOTHY. I'm old fashioned enough to want to be working. And now that the strike's on, whatever will I do? Well, Bert is after giving his life for human liberty,—the only thing a great-hearted country like America would be fighting for. There's some comfort in that! I think of him as a little boy, like when he'd be carrying me dinner pail to the shops at noon, runnin' and leppin' and callin' out to me, and he only that high!

ASHER. As a little boy!

TIMOTHY. Yes, sir, it's when I like to think of him best. There's a great comfort in childher, and when they grow up we lose them anyway. But it's fair beset I'll be now, with nothing to do but think of him.

ASHER. You can thank these scoundrels who are making this labour trouble for that.

TIMOTHY. Scoundrels, is it? Scoundrels is a hard word, Mr. Pindar.

ASHER. What else are they? Scoundrels and traitors! Don't tell me that you've gone over to them, Timothy—that you've deserted me, too! That you sympathize with these agitators who incite class against class!

TIMOTHY. I've heard some of them saying, sir, that if the unions gain what they're after, there'll be no classes at all at all. And classes is what some of us didn't expect to find in this country, but freedom.

ASHER. Freedom! They're headed for anarchy. And they haven't an ounce of patriotism.

TIMOTHY (meaningly). Don't say that, sir. Me own boy is after dying over there, and plenty have gone out of your own shops, as ye can see for yourself every time you pass under the office door with some of the stars in the flag turning to gold. And those who stays at home and works through the night is patriots, too. The unions may be no better than they should be, but the working man isn't wanting anyone to tell him whether he'd be joining them or not.

ASHER. I never expected to hear you talk like this!

TIMOTHY. Nor I, sir. But it's the sons, Mr. Pindar,—the childher that changes us. I've been thinking this morning that Bert had a union card in his pocket when he went away,—and if he died for that kind of liberty, it's good enough for his old father to live for. I see how wicked it was to be old fashioned.

ASHER. Wicked?

TIMOTHY. Isn't it the old fashioned nation we're fighting, with its kings and emperors and generals that would crush the life and freedom out of them that need life. And why wouldn't the men have the right to organize, sir, the way that they'd have a word to say about what they'd be doing?

ASHER. You—you ask me to sacrifice my principles and yield to men who are deliberately obstructing the war?

TIMOTHY. Often times principles is nothing but pride, sir. And it might be yourself that's obstructing the war, when with a simple word from you they'd go on working.

ASHER (agitatedly). I can't, I won't recognize a labour union!

TIMOTHY. Have patience, sir. I know ye've a kind heart, and that ye've always acted according to your light, the same as me. But there's more light now, sir,—it's shining through the darkness, brighter than the flashes of the cannon over there. In the moulding room just now it seems to break all around me, and me crying like a child because the boy was gone. There was things I hadn't seen before or if I saw them, it was only dim-like, to trouble me (ASHER turns away) the same as you are troubled now. And to think it's me that would pity you, Mr. Pindar! I says to myself, I'll talk to him. I ain't got no learning, I can't find the words I'm after—but maybe I can persuade him it ain't the same world we're living in.

ASHER. I was ready to recognize that. Before they came to me this morning I had made a plan to reorganize the shops, to grant many privileges.

TIMOTHY. You'll excuse me, sir, but it's what they don't want,—anyone to be granting them privileges, but to stand on their own feet, the same as you. I never rightly understood until just now,—and that because I was always looking up, while you'd be looking down, and seeing nothing but the bent backs of them. It's inside we must be looking, sir,—and God made us all the same, you and me, and Mr. George and my son Bert, and the Polak and his wife and childher. It's the strike in every one of us, sir,—and half the time we'd not know why we're striking!

ASHER. You're right there, Timothy

TIMOTHY. But that makes no difference, sir. It's what we can't be

reasoning, but the nature in us all—

(He flings his arm toward the open windows.)

—like the flowers and the trees in the doctor's garden groping to the

light of the sun. Maybe the one'll die for lack of the proper soil, and

many is cruelly trampled on, but the rest'll be growing, and none to

stop 'em.

ASHER (pacing to the end of the room, and turning). No, I won't listen to it! You— you ask me to yield to them, when you have lost your son, when they're willing to sacrifice—to murder my son on the field of battle?

(He pauses and looks toward the doorway, right. DR. JONATHAN

standing there, holding in his hand a yellow envelope. ASHER

starts forward.)

A telegram? For me?

DR. JONATHAN. Yes, Asher.

(After giving it to ASHER, DR. JONATHAN takes his stand beside

MINNIE, who is at the back of the room, near the bench. He lays a

hand on her arm. ASHER tears open the envelope and stares at the

telegram, his hands trembling.)

ASHER (exclaiming, in a half whisper). George!

AUGUSTA. Oh Asher, not—not—!

(She reaches for the telegram. He gives it to her. She reads.)

"Captain George Pindar severely wounded, condition critical."

TIMOTHY. Please God he'll be spared to ye!

    CURTAIN.

ACT III

SCENE: Same as in Act I, the library of ASHER PINDAR'S house.

TIME: The following day, early afternoon. A storm is raging, with wind

and rain and occasional bright flashes of lightning and heavy peals

of thunder. ASHER is pacing up and down the room, folding and

unfolding his hands behind his back, when AUGUSTA enters, lower

right, her knitting in her hand. There is a flash and a peal of

thunder.

AUGUSTA. Oh! Asher, did you know that the elm at the end of the Common was struck just now?—that splendid old landmark!

ASHER. All the old landmarks are being struck down, one after another.

AUGUSTA (going up to him and putting her hand on his arm). I've been so nervous all day. Do be careful how you go about during this strike. Those sullen and angry groups of men on the street this morning—

ASHER. Oh, they wouldn't dare touch me. If we only had a state constabulary we'd soon break that sort of thing up. But the Legislature trembles whenever a labour leader opens his mouth.

AUGUSTA (sitting down and taking up her knitting). If only I could be of some help to you! But it's always been so.

ASHER. You've been a good wife, Augusta!

AUGUSTA. I don't know. I've kept your house, I've seen that you were well fed, but I've been thinking lately how little that is for a woman—for a human being.

ASHER (surprised). Why, Augusta! I can't remember the time when you haven't been busy. You've taken an active part in church work and looked out for the people of the village.

AUGUSTA. Yes, and what has it all amounted to? The poor are ungrateful, they won't go near the church, and today they're buying pianos. Soon there won't be any poor to help.

ASHER. That's so. We'll be the paupers, if this sort of thing keeps on.

AUGUSTA. I've tried to do my duty as a Christian woman, but the world has no use, apparently, for Christians in these times. And whenever you have any really serious trouble, I seem to be the last person you take into your confidence.

ASHER. I don't worry you with business matters.

AUGUSTA. Because you do not regard me as your intellectual equal.

ASHER. A woman has her sphere. You have always filled it admirably.

AUGUSTA. "Adorn" is the word, I believe.

ASHER. To hear you talk, one would think you'd been contaminated by Jonathan. You, of all people!

AUGUSTA. There seems to be no place for a woman like me in these days,—I don't recognize the world I'm living in.

ASHER. You didn't sleep a wink last night, thinking of George.

AUGUSTA. I've given up all hope of ever seeing him again alive.

(Enter DR. JONATHAN, lower right. His calmness is in contrast to

the storm, and to the mental states of ASHER and AUGUSTA.)

Why, Jonathan, what are you doing out in this storm?

DR. JONATHAN. I came to see you, Augusta.

AUGUSTA (knitting, trying to hide her perturbation at his appearance). Did you? You might have waited until the worst was over. You still have to be careful of your health, you know.

DR. JONATHAN (sitting down). There are other things more important than my health. No later news about George, I suppose.

ASHER. Yes. I got another telegram early this morning saying that he is on his way home on a transport.

DR. JONATHAN. On his way home!

ASHER. If he lives to arrive. I'll show you the wire. Apparently they can't make anything out of his condition, but think it's shell shock. This storm has been raging along the coast ever since nine o'clock, the wires are down, but I did manage to telephone to New York and get hold of Frye, the shell-shock specialist. In case George should land today, he'll meet him.

DR. JONATHAN. Frye is a good man.

ASHER. George is hit by a shell and almost killed nearly a month ago, and not a word do I hear of it until I get that message in your house yesterday! Then comes this other telegram this morning. What's to be said about a government capable of such inefficiency? Of course the chances of his landing today are small, but I can't leave for New York until tonight because that same government sends a labour investigator here to pry into my affairs, and make a preliminary report. They're going to decide whether or not I shall keep my property or hand it over to them! And whom do they send? Not a business man, who's had practical experience with labour, but a professor out of some university,—a theorist!

DR. JONATHAN. Awkward people, these professors. But what would you do about it, Asher? Wall up the universities?

ASHER. Their trustees, who are business men, should forbid professors meddling in government and politics. This fellow had the impudence to tell me to my face that my own workmen, whom I am paying, aren't working for me. I'm only supposed to be supplying the capital. We talk about Germany being an autocracy it's nothing to what this country has become!

DR. JONATHAN (smiling). An autocracy of professors instead of business men. Well, every dog has his day. And George is coming home.

ASHER. And what is there left to hand over to him if he lives? What future has the Pindar Shops,—which I have spent my life to build up?

DR. JONATHAN. If George lives, as we hope, you need not worry about the future of the Pindar Shops, I think.

AUGUSTA. If God will only spare him!

ASHER. I guess I've about got to the point where I don't believe that a God exists.

(A flash and a loud peal of thunder.)

AUGUSTA. Asher

ASHER. Then let Him strike me!

(He hurries abruptly out of the door, left.)

AUGUSTA (after a silence). During all the years of our married life, he has never said such a thing as that. Asher an atheist!

DR. JONATHAN. So was Job, Augusta,—for a while.

AUGUSTA (avoiding DR. JONATHAN'S glance, and beginning to knit). You wanted to speak to me, Jonathan?

(The MAID enters, lower right.)

MAID. Timothy Farrell, ma'am.

(Exit maid, enter TIMOTHY FARRELL.)

AUGUSTA. I'm afraid Mr. Pindar can't see you just now, Timothy.

TIMOTHY. It's you I've come to see, ma'am, if you'll bear with me,—who once took an interest in Minnie.

AUGUSTA. It is true that I once took an interest in her, Timothy, but I'm afraid I have lost it. I dislike to say this to you, her father, but it's so.

TIMOTHY. Don't be hard on her, Mrs. Pindar. She may have been wild-like in Newcastle, but since she was back here to work for the doctor she's been a good girl, and that happy I wouldn't know her, and a comfort to me in me old age,—what with

Bert gone, and Jamesy taken to drink! And now she's run away and left me alone entirely, with the shops closed, and no work to do.

AUGUSTA (knitting). She's left Foxon Falls?

TIMOTHY (breaking down for a moment). When I woke up this morning I found a letter beside me bed—I'm not to worry, she says and I know how fond of me she was—be the care she took of me. She's been keeping company with no young man— that I know. If she wasn't working with the doctor on that discovery she'd be home with me.

AUGUSTA. I'm sorry for you, Timothy, but I don't see what I can do.

TIMOTHY. I minded that you were talking to her yesterday in the lab'rat'ry, before the telegram came about Mr. George.

AUGUSTA. Well?

TIMOTHY. It was just a hope, ma'am, catching at a straw-like.

AUGUSTA (tightening her lips). I repeat that I'm sorry for you, Timothy. I have no idea where she has gone.

TIMOTHY (looking at her fixedly. She pauses in her knitting and returns his look). Very well, ma'am—there's no need of my bothering you. You've heard nothing more of Mr. George?

AUGUSTA (with sudden tears). They're sending him home.

TIMOTHY. And now that ye're getting him back, ma'am, ye might think with a little more charity of her that belongs to me—the only one I'd have left.

(TIMOTHY goes out, lower right. AUGUSTA is blinded by tears. She

lets fall her ball of wool. DR. JONATHAN picks it up.)

AUGUSTA. I try to be fair in my judgments, and true to my convictions, but what Minnie has done cannot be condoned.

DR. JONATHAN (sitting down beside AUGUSTA) And what has Minnie done, Augusta?

AUGUSTA. You ask me that? I try hard to give you credit, Jonathan, for not knowing the ways of the world—but it's always been difficult to believe that Minnie Farrell had become well—a bad woman.

DR. JONATHAN. A bad woman. I gather, then, that you don't believe in the Christian doctrines of repentance and regeneration.

AUGUSTA (bridling). The leopard doesn't change his spots. And has she shown any sign of repentance? Has she come to me and asked my pardon for the way in which she treated me? Has she gone to church and asked God's forgiveness? But I know you are an agnostic, Jonathan,—it grieves me. I couldn't expect you to see the necessity of that.

DR. JONATHAN. If it hadn't been for Minnie, I shouldn't have been able to achieve a discovery that may prove of value to our suffering soldiers, as well as to injured operatives in factories. In spite of the news of her brother's death, Minnie worked all afternoon and evening. It was midnight when we made the successful test, after eight months of experiment.

AUGUSTA. I hope the discovery may be valuable. It seems to me that there is too much science in these days and too little religion. I've never denied that the girl is clever.

DR. JONATHAN. But you would deny her the opportunity to make something of her cleverness because in your opinion; she has broken the Seventh Commandment. Is that it?

AUGUSTA. I can't listen to you when you talk in this way.

DR. JONATHAN. But you listen every Sunday to Moses—if it was Moses?—when he talks in this way. You have made up your mind, haven't you, that Minnie has broken the Commandment?

AUGUSTA. I'm not a fool, Jonathan.

DR. JONATHAN. You are what is called a good woman. Have you proof that Minnie is what you would call a bad one?

AUGUSTA. Has she ever denied it? And you heard her when she stood up in this room and spoke of her life in Newcastle.

DR. JONATHAN. But no court of law would convict her on that.

AUGUSTA. And she had an affair with George. Oh, I can't talk about it!

DR. JONATHAN. I'm afraid that George will wish to talk about it, when he comes back.

AUGUSTA, She's been corresponding with George—scheming behind my back.

DR. JONATHAN. Are you sure of that?

AUGUSTA. She confessed to me that she had had letters from him.

DR. JONATHAN. And that she'd written letters in return?

AUGUSTA. What right have you to catechize me, Jonathan?

DR. JONATHAN. The same right, Augusta, that you have to catechize Minnie. Only I wish to discover the truth, and apparently you do not. She left me a letter, too, in which she said, "Don't try to find me—I wouldn't come back if you did. Mrs. Pindar was right about me, after all—I had to break loose again." Now, Augusta, I'd like to know what you make of that?

AUGUSTA. It's pretty plain, isn't it?

DR. JONATHAN. If the girl were really "bad," as you insist, would she say a thing like that?

AUGUSTA. I'm afraid I'm not an authority on Minnie's kind.

DR. JONATHAN. Well, I am. The only motive which could have induced her to leave my laboratory and Foxon Falls—her father—is what you would call a Christian motive.

AUGUSTA. What do you mean?

DR. JONATHAN. An unselfish motive. She went because she thought she could help someone by going.

AUGUSTA. Why—do you discuss this with me?

DR. JONATHAN. Because I've come to the conclusion that you know something about Minnie's departure, Augusta.

AUGUSTA (again on the verge of tears). Well, then, I do. I am responsible for her going—I'm not ashamed of it. Her remaining here was an affront to all right thinking people. I appealed to her, and she had the decency to leave.

DR. JONATHAN. Decency is a mild word to apply to her sacrifice.

AUGUSTA. I suppose, with your extraordinary radical views, you mean that she might have remained here and married George. One never can predict the harm that a woman of that kind can do.

DR. JONATHAN (rising). The harm that a bad woman can do, Augusta, is sometimes exceeded only by the harm a good woman can do. You are unfortunately steeped in a religion which lacks the faith in humanity that should be its foundation. The girl has just given you the strongest proof of an inherent goodness, and you choose to call her bad. But if you will not listen to Moses and the prophets, how will you listen to Christ?

AUGUSTA. Jonathan! Where are you going?

DR. JONATHAN. To find Minnie Farrell and bring her back to Foxon Falls.

(He goes out, lower right. AUGUSTA sits for a while, motionless,

and then makes an attempt to go on with her knitting. A man's face

is seen pressed against the glass of the middle window. AUGUSTA

does not perceive him. He disappears, the glass door, upper right,

opens slowly and PRAG enters! His clothes are wet, he is unshaven,

he is gaunt and ill, and his eyed gleans. He leaves the door open

behind him. Once inside the room, he halts and stares at AUGUSTA,

who gathers up her knitting and rises. She does not lack courage.)

AUGUSTA. What do you want?

PRAG. I come to see Mr. Pindar.

AUGUSTA. The proper place to see Mr. Pindar is in his office. What do you mean by forcing your way into this house?

PRAG (advancing). I have no right here—it is too fine for me, yes?

(Through the window the figure of a woman is seen running across the

lawn, and a moment later MINNIE FARRELL comes in through the open

doorway, upper right. She is breathless and somewhat wet.)

AUGUSTA. Minnie!

PRAG (turning and confronting MINNIE). So! You come back to Foxon Falls, too!

MINNIE. You guessed it.

PRAG. You follow me?

MINNIE. But you're some sprinter! (She seizes him by the arm.) Come on, Prag,—you haven't got any business here, and you know it.

PRAG (stubbornly). I come to see Mr. Pindar. I vill see him!

AUGUSTA. He isn't home.

PRAG. Then I vait for him.

MINNIE (glancing toward the study door, where she suspects ASHER is). No you don't, either! You come along with me.

(She pulls him, and he resists. They begin to struggle. AUGUSTA

cries out and runs to MINNIE's assistance.)

Keep away, Mrs. Pindar. If Mr. Pindar's home, find him and tell him not to come in here. This man's crazy.

PRAG (struggling with MINNIE). Crazy, is it? What is it to you—what I do with Mr. Pindar. He is also your enemy—the enemy of all work-peoples.

(AUGUSTA, after a second's indecision, turns and runs toward the

door, left, that leads into ASHER's study. MINNIE tries to push

PRAG toward the doorway, upper right, but she is no match for the

nervous strength he is able to summon up in his fanatical frenzy.

Just as AUGUSTA reaches the study door, it is flung open and ASHER

appears.)

ASHER. What's the matter?

(Then he sees MINNIE and PRAG struggling and strides toward them.

AUGUSTA tries to prevent him reaching them. PRAG wrenches himself

free from MINNIE and draws a pistol front his pocket. MINNIE flings

herself between him and ASHER, who momentarily halts, too astonished

to act.)

PRAG (to MINNIE). Get avay! He kill my wife, he drive me out of my home—he will not have the unions. I shoot him! Get oudt!

ASHER. Stand aside, Minnie, I'll take care of him.

(AUGUSTA cries out. ASHER advances, seizes MINNIE by the shoulder

and thrusts her aside. PRAG has the pistol levelled at him.)

PRAG. Recognize the unions, or I shoot!

ASHER. Lower that pistol! Do you think you can intimidate me?

PRAG. They can hang me,—I die for freedoms!

(He is apparently about to pull the trigger, but he does not. His

eyes are drawn away from ASHER, toward the doorway, lower right,

where DR. JONATHAN is seen standing, gazing at him. Gradually his

arm drops to his side, and DR. JONATHAN goes up to him and takes the

pistol from his hand. PRAG breaks down, sobbing violently.)

It is no good! I can't—now.

DR. JONATHAN (his hand on PRAG'S shoulder). Come with me, Prag, to my house.

(He leads PRAG, shaken by sobs, out of the doorway, upper right,

and they are seen through the windows crossing the lawn and

disappearing.)

AUGUSTA. Oh, Asher!

(She goes up to him and puts her hand on his arm, and then turns to

MINNIE.)

You saved him

MINNIE. Dr. Jonathan saved him. He'd save everybody, if they'd let him. Ever since he took care of Prag's wife, when she died, he's got him hypnotized.

ASHER. You've done a brave thing, Minnie. I shan't forget it.

MINNIE. I want you to forget it. I wouldn't like to see anybody hurt.

AUGUSTA. But—how did you happen to be here—in Foxon Falls?

MINNIE. Oh, I didn't mean to come back. I'm going away again.

AUGUSTA. I have no right to ask you to go away, now.

ASHER. What's this? Did you ask Minnie to leave Foxon Falls?

AUGUSTA. Asher, I'd like to talk with Minnie, if you don't mind.

ASHER (glancing at the two women). Well, I shan't forget what you've done, Minnie.

(He goes out, lower right.)

MINNIE (who is on the verge of losing her self-control). I didn't come back to Foxon Falls to talk to you again, Mrs. Pindar. I'm sorry, but I've got to go.

AUGUSTA. Where?

MINNIE. You didn't care yesterday—why should you care today?

AUGUSTA (with an effort). I ought to tell you that Dr. Pindar has declined Mr. Pindar's offer.

MINNIE. He isn't going to take charge of the hospital?

AUGUSTA. No.

MINNIE. But if he's so poor, how's he going to live? He can't afford to hire me to help him.

AUGUSTA. I don't know. Dr. Pindar was about to leave in search of you.

MINNIE. I was afraid of that—when he ought to be going to New York to test the discovery at the hospitals there. He meant to.

AUGUSTA. You must see him.

MINNIE. Oh, I'll see him now. That was what hurt me most, lying to him about why I was leaving—letting him think I was sick of working with him.

AUGUSTA. Minnie, I'm willing to say that I was mistaken about you. You may have been unwise, but you never did anything wrong. Isn't it so?

MINNIE. Why do you think that now? What changed you? Just because I might have helped to keep Mr. Pindar from being shot by a crazy man—that didn't change you, did it?

AUGUSTA. I was mistaken!

MINNIE. If you thought I was bad yesterday, I'm bad today.

AUGUSTA. A bad woman couldn't have done what you did just now.

MINNIE. Don't you believe it, Mrs. Pindar. I knew a woman in Newcastle—but there's no use going into that, I guess. There's worse kinds of badness than what you call bad.

AUGUSTA. I—I can't discuss it. But I want to be just. I'm convinced that I did you a wrong—and I'm sorry. Won't you believe me?

MINNIE. But you'll never forgive me—even if I hadn't done what you thought—on account of what happened with George.

AUGUSTA. I—I'll try.

MINNIE. No, don't try—forgiveness doesn't come that way, Mrs. Pindar. (With sudden acuteness.) It was on account of George, not Dr. Jonathan, that you wanted to get me out of Foxon Falls.

AUGUSTA. I repeat—I shouldn't have asked you to go. Isn't that enough?

MINNIE. I told you not to worry about me and George. I ran away from him once— I guess I won't have to do it again.

AUGUSTA. You—you ran away from him?

MINNIE. From the church, too, and from the Bible class and from you, and from the shops. But I'm free now, there isn't any danger of my going wrong,—I know what I can do, I've learned my job—Dr. Jonathan's taught me. You needn't have me on your conscience, either. I'll go across and see if I can help Dr. Jonathan take care of that poor wreck, Prag. Life's been too tough for him—

AUGUSTA (starting forward to detain her). Wait a moment, Minnie,—tell me how you happened to come back, to be here so—providentially.

MINNIE. There wasn't anything providential about it. I took the six o'clock train to Newcastle this morning. Not that I had any notion of staying there. I ran into Prag at the station. I nursed his wife, you know—and he started in to tell me how he was coming up to Foxon Falls to shoot Mr. Pindar because he'd closed down the works rather than recognize the union. I knew that Prag was just about crazy enough to do it, because I've heard Dr. Jonathan talk about the mental disease he's got. That was about ten, and the train for Foxon Falls was leaving in a few minutes. I ran into the booth to phone Dr. Jonathan, but the storm had begun down there, and I couldn't get a connection. So I caught the train, and when it pulled in here I saw Pray jump out of the smoking car and start to run. I couldn't run as fast as he could, and I'd only got to the other side of the Common when I saw him walk into the house.

AUGUSTA (after a pause). Minnie, you'll stay here now? Your father needs you—I—I should never forgive myself if you left.

MINNIE. Tell me, Mrs. Pindar,—have you heard anything more from George?

AUGUSTA (hesitating). Yes—Mr. Pindar got a telegram this morning.

MINNIE. He's coming home! When will he get here?

AUGUSTA. I—don't know. Oh, I'm afraid he may never get here—alive.

MINNIE. Don't say that! George will live—he's got to live.

AUGUSTA (gazing, at her). What makes you think so?

MINNIE. Because he's needed so in the world—in Foxon Falls.

(She starts for the doorway, upper right.)

AUGUSTA. You're not going?

MINNIE. I couldn't stay here—now.

AUGUSTA. Why—why not?

MINNIE (in tears). I should think you'd know why not!

AUGUSTA. You mean—you care—you care that much?

85

MINNIE. I'm going.

(She turns to leave the room when the sound of an automobile is

heard without, the brakes going on, etc. MINNIE, who has got as far

as the doorway, upper right halts and stares.)

AUGUSTA (excitedly). What is it?

MINNIE. An automobile. Oh, Mrs. Pindar—it's him—it's George!

(She draws back from the doorway, her hands clasped.)

AUGUSTA. George! (She hurries toward the doorway, speaking as she goes.) Where is he?

Why doesn't he come in?

MINNIE (staring out). He can't. Oh, I'll get Dr. Jonathan!

(She is speaking as AUGUSTA goes out.)

(Mingling with other voices, ASHER's resonant and commanding voice

is heard.)

ASHER (without). Bring him in through the library—it's easier for you, George.

(MINNIE who obviously cannot now escape through the doorway, upper

right, without GEORGE seeing her, after a second's resolution dashes

across the room and out of the door, lower right. A moment later

GEORGE is brought in through the doorway, upper right, leaning

heavily on Dr. FRYE, a capable looking man, whose well fitting

business suit and general appearance indicate a prosperous city practice. GEORGE is in uniform. He is much thinner, and his face

betrays acute suffering. His left arm hangs helpless at his side.)

(ASHER and AUGUSTA follow, ASHER with a look of pain which has been

increased by an incident which occurred at the automobile, where

GEORGE refused to allow ASHER to help support him.)

(GEORGE gets a little way into the room when he stops, sways a

little, and spasmodically puts his hand to his heart. ASHER, in a

frenzy of anxiety, again approaches to help him, but GEORGE repulses

him.)

GEORGE (protesting with what strength he has, as if in fear). N—no, dad, I'd rather not—I—I can get along.

(ASHER halts and gazes at him mutely, and then looks at AUGUSTA.)

DR. FRYE. You'd better sit down here a minute and rest, Captain Pindar.

(ASHER starts to pull up an armchair, but AUGUSTA looks at him and

shakes her head, and pulls it up herself. GEORGE sinks into the

chair, leans back his head and closes his eyes. AUGUSTA hovers over

him, smoothing his hair.)

AUGUSTA. Is there nothing we can do, Dr. Frye? A little brandy—?

Dr. FRYE (who is evidently trying to hide his own concern by a show of professional self-confidence), I think I'd wait a few moments.

GEORGE (murmuring). I—I'll be all right, mother

(DR. FRYE stands gazing down at him a few seconds and then comes

forward into the room to join ASHER.)

ASHER. For God's sake tell me what it is, doctor! Why did you leave New York with him when he was in this condition? Was it because?

Dr. FRYE (speaking more rapidly than is his wont). He was surprisingly well, considering everything, when we left New York, and the army medical men advised taking him home. I thought an automobile better than a slow train. I tried to telephone you, but the storm—

ASHER. I know.

Dr. FRYE. I sent you a wire.

ASHER. I didn't get it.

DR. FRYE. It was impossible to get a good nurse on account of the influenza epidemic. In fact, I didn't think he needed one—but I thought you'd feel more comfortable if I came. He seemed extraordinary well, even cheerful until we got right into Foxon Falls. We were passing your shops, and a big crowd of men were there, making a noise, shouting at a speaker. Is there a strike on here?

ASHER. Yes. You say he got like this when he saw the crowd?

DR. FRYE (indicating GEORGE). As you see. He fell back on the cushions as though he'd been hit—it all happened in a second. I have the history of the case from the army people—he had an attack something like this abroad.

ASHER. Did you notice how he avoided me?

DR. FRYE (with reluctance). That may not be anything. It's his heart, at present,— and yet I'm convinced that this is a case for a psychologist as well as for a medical man. I confess I'm puzzled, and as soon as we can get a connection with New York I want to summon Barnwell.

ASHER. I'll see if I can get a wire through.

DR. FRYE. Telephone Plaza 4632.

(ASHER hurries out, lower right. Dr. FRYE returns to GEORGE to take

his pulse when DR. JONATHAN enters, upper right. He crosses the

room directly to GEORGE and stands looking down at him.)

AUGUSTA (who is a little behind GEORGE'S chair, gives DR. JONATHAN an agonized glance, which she transfers to Dr. FRYE when he drops GEORGE'S wrist). George! George, dear!

(DR. FRYE is silent Then ASHER reenters.)

ASHER (in a low tone, to Dr. FRYE). They think they can get New York within half an hour.

(DR. FRYE nods. His attention is now fixed upon DR. JONATHAN, whose

gaze is still focussed on GEORGE. ASHER and AUGUSTA now begin to

look at DR. JONATHAN. Gradually, as though by the compulsion of DR.

JONATHAN'S regard; GEORGE slowly opens his eyes.)

GEORGE (stammering). Dr. Jonathan!

DR. JONATHAN. I'm here, George.

GEORGE. Is there-is there a strike in the shops?

(DR. JONATHAN glances at ASHER.)

ASHER (hesitating, speaking with difficulty). Don't worry about that now, George.

GEORGE. Why—why are they striking?

ASHER. I'll tell you all about it later—when you feel better.

GEORGE (feebly, yet insistent). I—I want to know.

ASHER. We can't talk about it now, my boy—later.

GEORGE. Did—did you get my letter—the letter in which I begged you—

ASHER. Yes, yes—I'll explain it all tomorrow.

GEORGE. I—I may not be here—tomorrow. You didn't do what—I asked? It's—so simple—when you've thought about it—when you've fought for it.

ASHER. I—I had a plan, George. We'll go over it

(He approaches GEORGE.)

GEORGE (shrinking). No—no!

(ASHER recoils. MINNIE FARRELL appears, upper right, from the

direction of the Common. She carries a phial, a dropper and some

water in a glass. Seeing the group gathered about GEORGE, she

hesitates, but DR. JONATHAN motions her to come forward.)

W—who is that? Minnie?

(GEORGE makes an attempt to sit up, but his head falls back and his

eyes close again. Then DR. JONATHAN lays his hand on Dr. FRYE's

arm, as though to draw him aside.)

Dr. FRYE. Is this Dr. Jonathan Pindar? I wondered if you were a relation—(he glances at ASHER)—but I wasn't looking for you in Foxon Falls. If you have something to suggest—?

DR. JONATHAN (taking the phial and the dropper from MINNIE). With your permission. In any case it can do no harm.

DR. FRYE. By all means: If I had realized you were here—!

(ASHER looks on in astonishment. DR. JONATHAN measures out a few

drops of the liquid from the phial into the glass of water, which

MINNIE holds.)

DR. JONATHAN. George, will you take this?

(He holds the glass while GEORGE drinks. To Dr. FRYE:)

There's a lounge in Mr. Pindar's study.

(To AUGUSTA:) Get a blanket.

(AUGUSTA goes toward the door, lower right, while MINNIE Starts to

retire.)

We'll need you, Minnie.

(He hands MINNIE the glass, dropper and phial. The two physicians

pick GEORGE up and carry him out, left, followed by MINNIE. ASHER

goes a little way and then halts with a despairing gesture. AUGUSTA

having gone for the blanket, ASHER is left alone, pacing, until she

returns.)

AUGUSTA (going through the room from right to left, with the blanket). Ah, Asher!

(ASHER begins pacing again, when Dr. FRYE reenters from the left.)

ASHER. Is there—is there any hope?

DR. FRYE (his hand on ASHER'S sleeve). I can tell you more when I have had a chance to talk with Dr. Pindar. This seems to be one of his cases—but I confess, when I mentioned Barnwell, I didn't think of him. The situation came so suddenly. And in spite of his name being yours, I didn't expect to find him here.

ASHER. Then you know of Jonathan?

DR. FRYE. I didn't know of him until I read the book which he published about a year ago. When I was in Baltimore in March, I asked for him at Johns Hopkins's, and they told me that he had gone to New England for his health. Extraordinary to meet him here—and today!

ASHER. What book? He's never spoken to me of any book.

DR. FRYE. On the Physical Effects of Mental Crises. There has been a good deal of controversy about it in the profession, but I'm one of those who believe that the physician must seek to cure, not only the body, but the soul. We make a guess— though he's published no religion—the true scientist is the minister of the future.

ASHER. I never realized that Jonathan—!

DR. FRYE (smiling a little). No prophet is without honour save in his own country.

ASHER. What has he given George?

DR. FRYE. I can't tell you exactly, but I can make a guess—though he's published no account of his recent experiments.

(As DR. JONATHAN reenters from the left.)

He will undoubtedly tell you himself. (Exit Dr. FRYE, left.)

ASHER. Will he live?

DR. JONATHAN. I'll be frank with you, Asher,—I don't know. All we can do is to wait.

ASHER. I call God to witness there's nothing I wouldn't do, no sacrifice I wouldn't make, if that boy could be saved!

DR. JONATHAN. Remember that, Asher.

ASHER. Remember what?

DR. JONATHAN. If his life is saved, you will be called upon to make a sacrifice, to do your part.

ASHER. My part?

DR. JONATHAN. Yes. What I have given him—the medicine—is only half the battle—should it succeed. My laboratory experiments were only completed last night.

ASHER. This is what you have been working on?

DR. JONATHAN. It happens to be. But I have had no chance to test it—except on animals. I meant to have gone to a war hospital in New York today. If it works, then we shall have to try the rest of the experiment,—your half of it.

ASHER. What's that?

DR. JONATHAN. You probably noticed that George avoided you.

ASHER. It's more than I can bear. You know what we've been to each other. If he should die—feeling that way—!

DR. JONATHAN. George hasn't lost his affection for you; if it were so, we shouldn't have that symptom. I will tell you, briefly, my theory of the case. But first let me say, in justice to Frye, that he was in no position to know certain facts that give the clue to George's condition the mental history.

ASHER. I don't understand.

DR. JONATHAN. The day he left home, for France, certain things happened to him to arouse his sympathy with what we call working people, their lives and aspirations. As you know, George has a very human side,—he loves his fellow men. He'd never thought of these things before. He went with them, naturally, to you, and I infer that you suppressed him!

ASHER. I told him I couldn't discuss certain aspects. His emotional state troubled me,—he was going away, and I imagined he would get over it.

DR. JONATHAN. He didn't get over it. It was an emotional crisis. He left home with a conflict in his mind,—a conflict between his affection for you and that which he had suddenly come to see was right. I mean, right for today, for the year and hour in which we are living. This question of the emancipation of labour began a hundred years ago, with the introduction of machinery and the rise of modern industry, and in this war it has come to a head. Well, as the time approached for George to risk his life for his new beliefs, his mental conflict deepened. He talked with other young men who believed they were fighting for the same cause. And then—it must have been shortly before he was wounded—he wrote you that appeal.

ASHER. The letter I read to you!

DR. JONATHAN. The fact that in his own home, in the shops which bore his name, no attempt had been made to meet the new issues for which he was going into battle, weighed upon him. Then came the shell that shattered his body. But the probabilities are that he was struck down, unconscious, at the very moment when the conflict in his mind was most acute. He was thinking of you, of the difference you and he had had, he was lonely, he was afraid for the bravest men feel fear. To him the bursting of the shell was the bursting of the conflict within him. I won't go into the professional side of the matter, the influence of the mental state on the physical—but after the wound healed, whenever anything occurred to remind him of the conflict,—a letter from you, the sight of the strikers this afternoon at the shops, meeting you once more, a repetition came of what happened when the shell struck him. Certain glands fail in their functions, the heart threatens to stop and put an end to life. If my theory is correct, what I have given him may tide over that danger, but only on one condition can he continue to live and become a useful member of society.

ASHER. What condition?

DR. JONATHAN. That the mental conflict, the real cause of the trouble, he resolved. The time has come, Asher, when you must make your choice between your convictions and your son.

ASHER. Speak out.

DR. JONATHAN. I mean that you must be prepared to tell George, if he recovers, that you have abandoned your attitude toward the workmen, that you are willing to recognize their union, settle the strike, and go even further than in their ignorance they ask. You must try the experiment in the democratization of industry on which George's heart is set. Otherwise I will not answer for his sanity, I cannot even give you the hope that he will live.

ASHER. I never heard of a mental conflict producing such a state!

DR. JONATHAN. Remember, you have said that you will make any sacrifice to save George's life.

94

ASHER (turning on DR. JONATHAN). You're not trying to play on my—my superstition,—at a time like this!

DR. JONATHAN. I'm not dealing with superstition, Asher, but with science. If George revives, he will wish to talk with you.

ASHER. When?

DR. JONATHAN. Probably this evening—or never. I ask you the question—will you yield your convictions?

(ASHER bows his head. DR. JONATHAN gazes at him for a moment,

compassionately.)

I'll go back to him now. I think he'd better be moved to his room, and put to bed.

(Exit DR. JONATHAN, left. For a minute ASHER remains alone, and

then DR. JONATHAN and Dr. FRYE reappear, carrying GEORGE. The

blanket is flung over his knees, and he seems lifeless. They are

followed by MINNIE, carrying the phial and the glass, and by

AUGUSTA. They cross the room and go out, lower right. ASHER walks

behind them as far as the door, hesitates, and then goes out.)

(THE CURTAIN falls and remains down a minute to indicate a lapse of

three hours. When it rises again night has come, the lamps are

lighted and the window curtains drawn. ASHER and AUGUSTA are

discovered standing together. ASHER has a black, leather covered

book in his hand, with one finger in the place where he has been

reading. Both show the effects of a strain.)

AUGUSTA (who has been speaking). And when we took him upstairs, I was sure he was going to die—it seemed to me as if nothing could save him. He's been sitting up and talking to us—of course he's pale and weak and wasted, but in spite of that, Asher, he seems to have a strength, a force that he didn't have before he went away. He isn't a boy any more. I can't describe it, but I'm almost afraid of him—!

ASHER. He—he hasn't mentioned me?

AUGUSTA. No, my dear—and since Jonathan warned me not to, I've said nothing about you. Why is it?

ASHER. Jonathan's the master now.

AUGUSTA. In spite of what I've felt about him, he has saved George for us. It seems a miracle.

ASHER. A scientific miracle.

AUGUSTA (indicating the book ASHER holds). And yet you were reading the Bible!

ASHER. I just took it down. (He lays it on the table, and touches AUGUSTA, with an unwonted tenderness, on the shoulder). I think we may hope, now, Augusta. But before we can be sure that he'll get well, there's something else to be done.

AUGUSTA (anxiously). What?

ASHER. Go back to George,—I'll tell you later. It seems that we must trust Jonathan. Here he is now.

(Enter DR. JONATHAN, lower right, as AUGUSTA departs.)

DR. JONATHAN. George wants to get dressed, and come down.

ASHER. You think it wise?

DR. JONATHAN. Under the circumstances yes. The heart is practically normal again, we have done all that is physically possible. One half of the experiment seems to have succeeded, and the sooner we try the other half, the better. Are you still willing?

ASHER. I'm prepared. I've carried out your—instructions—sent for the committee.

DR. JONATHAN (looking at him). Good!

ASHER (with an effort). Jonathan, I—I guess I misjudged you—

DR. JONATHAN (Smiling). Wait until you are sure. Nothing matters if we can save that boy. By the way, he asked for Timothy, and I've sent for him.

ASHER. He asked for Timothy, and not for me!

DR. JONATHAN. It seems he saw an officer of Bert's regiment, after the boy was killed. Here's the committee, I think.

(The MAID enters, lower right. She does not speak, but ushers in

HILLMAN, RENCH and FERSEN, and retires.)

HILLMAN. | RENCH. |-Good evening, Mr. Pindar. Good evening, doctor.
FERSEN. |

ASHER. Good evening.

(An awkward silence. From habit, ASHER stares at them defiantly, as

DR. JONATHAN goes out, lower right.)

HILLMAN (going up to ASHER). How's your son, Mr. Pindar?

RENCH. We're real anxious about the Captain.

FERSEN (nodding). The boys think a whole lot of him, Mr. Pindar.

ASHER. He's better, thank you. The medicine Dr. Pindar has given him

RENCH. Didn't I say so? When I heard how he was when he got back, I said to Fred Hillman here,—if anybody can cure him, it's Dr. Jonathan, right here in Foxon Falls!

(A pause.)

I'm sorry this here difference came up just now, Mr. Pindar, when the Captain come home. We was a little mite harsh—but we was strung up, I guess, from the long shifts. If we'd known your son was comin'—

ASHER. You wouldn't have struck?

RENCH. We'd have agreed to put it off. When a young man like that is near dying for his country why—anything can wait. But what we're asking is only right.

ASHER. Well, right or not right, I sent for you to say, so far as I'm concerned, the strike's over.

RENCH. You'll—you'll recognize the union?

ASHER. I grant—(he catches himself)—I consent to your demands.

(After a moment of stupefaction, their faces light up, and they

approach him.)

RENCH. We appreciate it, Mr. Pindar. This'll make a lot of families happy tonight.

FERSEN. It will that.

HILLMAN. Maybe you won't believe me, Mr. Pindar, but it was hard to see the shops closed down—as hard on us as it was on you. We take pride in them, too. I guess you won't regret it.

ASHER (waving them away). I hope not. I ought to tell you that you may thank my son for this—my son and Dr. Pindar.

RENCH. We appreciate it,—just the same.

(ASHER makes a gesture as thought to dismiss the subject, as well as

the committee. They hesitate, and are about to leave when GEORGE,

followed by DR. JONATHAN, comes in, lower right. His entrance is

quite dramatic. He walks with the help of a stick, slowly, but his bearing is soldierly, authoritative, impressive. He halts when he

perceives the committee.)

HILLMAN (going up to GEORGE). How are you, Captain?

FERSEN. Good to have you home once more.

RENCH (going up to GEORGE). Good to see you, Captain, on a day like this. As Larz Fersen said when we were going to strike, "It's a fine day for it." Well, this is a better day—you home and well, and the strike off.

GEORGE (glancing from one to the other, and then at ASHER). What do you mean?

RENCH. Why, Mr. Pindar—your father here's just made everybody happy. He's recognized the union, and we're going back to work. We'll turn out machines to make shrapnel enough to kill every Hun in France,—get square with 'em for what they done to you.

(They all watch GEORGE, absorbed in the effect this announcement has

on him. An expression of happiness grows in his eyes. After a

moment he goes up to ASHER.)

GEORGE. Dad, why did you do this?

ASHER. I'll tell you, George. When you came home this afternoon I realized something I hadn't realized before. I saw that the tide was against me, that I was like that old English king who set his throne on the sands and thought he could stay the waters. If—if anything had happened to you, I couldn't have fought on, but now that you're here with me again, now that you've risked your life and almost lost it for this—this new order in which you believe, why, it's enough for me—I can surrender with honour. I'm tired, I need a rest. I'd have gone down fighting, but I guess you've saved me. I've been true to my convictions,—you, who belong to the new generation, must be true to yours. And as I told you once, all I care about this business is to hand it over to you.

GEORGE. You'll help me!

ASHER. This seems to be Jonathan's speciality,—science. But I never give my word half heartedly, my boy, and I'll back you to my last dollar. Be prepared for disappointments,—but if you accomplish something, I'll be glad. And if you fail, George,—any failure for a man's convictions is a grand failure.

GEORGE. Well, it means life to me, dad. I owe it to you.

ASHER (turning toward DR. JONATHAN). No, you owe it to him,—to science.

(He puts one hand on GEORGE'S shoulder, and the other, with an

abrupt movement, on DR. JONATHAN'S.)

And if science will do as much for democracy, then—

GEORGE. Then, you're from Missouri. Good old dad!

ASHER (huskily, trying, to carry it off, and almost overcome by emotion at the reconciliation). I'm from Missouri, my boy.

DR. JONATHAN. Then you're a true scientist, Asher, for science, too, waits to be shown.

(ASHER goes out, lower right. Dr. JONATHAN, evidently in support

and sympathy, goes with him. GEORGE and the committee look after

them, and then GEORGE sits down, and smiles at the men.)

GEORGE. And we've got to be scientists, too. Are you fellows willing to take your share in the experiment?

HILLMAN. What experiment's that, Captain?

GEORGE. Now that you've got your union, what's the good of it?

RENCH (after a pause). Why, I thought we'd made that pretty clear, Captain. We've got something to fall back on in case the employers don't live up to their agreements. I'm not speaking of you—

GEORGE. In other words, you've got a weapon.

RENCH. Well, you might call it that.

GEORGE. But weapons imply warfare,—don't they?

RENCH. We wouldn't fight with you.

GEORGE. Yes, you would,—if our interests conflicted. When I was in the trenches I kept thinking of the quotation Lincoln used, "A house divided against itself cannot stand." We're going to try to perpetuate that house, just as he did.

HILLMAN. Lincoln had common sense.

GEORGE. Another name for intelligence. And what we've got to decide is whether the old house will do—for democracy—industrial democracy? Can we shore up the timbers—or shall we have to begin to build a new house?

RENCH (glancing at HILLMAN). The old one sure enough looks rotten to me. I've said that all along.

GEORGE. It seems to have served its day. Has your union got the plans of a new house ready—consulted an architect?

RENCH. I'm afraid we don't get you, Captain.

GEORGE. You belong to the American Federation of Labour, don't you? Has it got a new house ready to move into?

RENCH. Well, I haven't seen any plans.

GEORGE. If the old structure's too small, one party or the other will have to be shoved out. The capitalist or the employee. Which will it be?

RENCH (laughing). If it comes to that—

GEORGE (smiling). There's no question in your mind. But you hadn't thought about it—your Federation hasn't thought about it, or doesn't want to think about it, and your employers don't want to, either.

HILLMAN (stroking his moustache). That's so

GEORGE. I'll tell you who have thought about it—the Bolshevists and the I. W. W. And because they have a programme,—some programme, any programme, they're more intelligent than we, for the time.

RENCH. Those guys?

GEORGE. Exactly,—those guys. At least they see that the house isn't fit to live in. They want to pull it down, and go back to living in trees and caves.

HILLMAN. That's about right.

GEORGE. But you're conservatives, you labour union people—the aristocrats of labour, which means that you don't think. What you really object to, when you come down to it, is that men like my father and me, and the bankers,—we're all in the same boat, most of 'us own banks, too,—control the conditions of life for you and men like you.

RENCH. I never heard it put in those words, but by gum, it's so.

GEORGE. And your Confederation, your unions are for the skilled workers, whose conditions aren't so bad,—and they're getting better every time you jack up the wages. You complain that we employers aren't thinking of you, but are you thinking of the millions of the unskilled who live from hand to mouth? The old structure's good enough for you, too. But what will the miserable men, who don't sit in, be doing while we're squabbling to see who'll have the best rooms?

RENCH. Blow the house up, I guess.

GEORGE. If they're rough with it, it'll tumble down like a pack of cards—simply because we're asses. Can't we build a house big enough for all—for a hundred million people and their descendants? A house in which, after a while, there will be no capitalists and no exploiters and no wreckers, only workers—each man and woman on the job they were fitted for? It's a man-sized job, but isn't it worth tackling?

RENCH (enthused). It's sure worth tackling, Captain.

GEORGE. And can't we begin it, in a modest way, by making a little model of the big house right here in Foxon Falls? Dr. Jonathan will help us.

RENCH. Go to it, Captain. We'll trust him and you.

GEORGE. Trust is all right, but you've got to go to it, too, and use your headpieces. We've got to sit down together and educate ourselves, who are now employers and employees, get hold of all the facts, the statistics,—and all the elements, the human nature side of it, from the theorists, the students, whom we've despised.

RENCH. Well, it's a fact, I hadn't thought much of them intellectuals.

GEORGE. They're part of the game—their theories are the basis for an intelligent practice. And what should we be able to do without their figures? Look at what we've worked out in large scale production and distribution in this war! That's a new world problem. Shall we be pioneers here in Foxon Falls in the new experiment?

RENCH. An experiment in human chemicals, as the doctor would say. Pioneers! I kind of like that word. You can put me in the wagon, Captain.

GEORGE. It will be a Conestoga with the curtains rolled up, so that everybody can see in. No secrets. And it will be a wagon with an industrial constitution.

FERSEN. Excuse me, Captain,—but what's that?

(RENCH laughs.)

GEORGE (smiling). Hasn't it struck you, Fersen, that unless a man has a voice and an interest in the industry in which he works his voice, and interest in the government for which he votes is a mockery?

(FERSEN nods.)

RENCH. We'll have to give Larz a little education.

GEORGE. Oh, I guess he'll make a good industrial citizen. But that's part of the bargain.

RENCH. That's fair. Human nature ain't so rotten, when you give it a chance.

GEORGE. Well, then, are you willing to try it out, on the level?

RENCH. I cal'late we'll stick, Captain.

HILLMAN. We sure will.

FERSEN. We'll be pioneers!

GEORGE. That's good American, Fersen, not to be afraid of an ideal. Shake! We'll sit down with it in a day or two.

(They all shake. The members of the committee file out of the room,

lower right. GEORGE is left alone for a brief interval, when

MINNIE, in the white costume of a nurse, enters, lower right,

with a glass of medicine in her hand.)

MINNIE (halting). You're all alone? Where's Dr. Jonathan?

GEORGE. He's gone off with dad.

MINNIE. It's nine o'clock.

(She hands him the glass, he drinks the contents and sets the glass

on the table. Then he takes her hands and draws her to him and

kisses her. She submits almost passively.)

Why are you doing this, George?

GEORGE. Because I love you, because I need you, because I'm going to marry you.

MINNIE (shaking her head: slowly). No you're not.

GEORGE. Why not?

MINNIE. You know why not, as well as I do.

(She gazes up at him. He is still holding her in his arms.

Suddenly she kisses him passionately, breaks away from him and

starts to fly from the room, when she runs into DR. JONATHAN, who is

entering, lower right.)

DR. JONATHAN. Where are you going, Minnie?

(MINNIE halts, and is silent. DR. JONATHAN lays a detaining hand on

her arm, and looks from one to the other, comprehendingly.)

GEORGE. I've asked her to marry me, Dr. Jonathan.

DR. JONATHAN. And what are your objections, Minnie?

MINNIE. You know why I can't, Dr. Jonathan. What kind of a wife would I make for him, with his family and friends. I'd do anything for him but that! He wouldn't be happy.

DR. JONATHAN. And what's your answer, George?

GEORGE. I don't want her for my family and friends,—I want her for myself. This isn't a snap judgment—I've had time to think it over.

MINNIE. I didn't mean to be here when you got home. I know I'm not fit to be your wife I haven't had any education.

GEORGE. Neither have I. We start level there. I've lived among people of culture, and I've found out that culture chiefly consists of fixed ideas, and obstruction to progress, of hating the President,—of knowing the right people and eating fish with a fork.

MINNIE (smiling, though in tears). Well, I never ate fish with a knife, anyway.

GEORGE. I spent my valuable youth learning Greek and Latin, and I can't speak or read either of them. I know that Horace wrote odes, and Cicero made orations, but I can't quote them. All I remember about biology is that the fittest are supposed to survive, and in this war I've seen the fittest killed off like flies. You've had several years of useful work in the Pindar Shops and the Wire Works, to say nothing of a course in biological chemistry, psychology and sociology under Dr. Jonathan. I'll leave it to him whether you don't know more about life than I do—about the life and problems of the great mass of people in this country. And now that the strike's over—

MINNIE. The strike's over!

105

GEORGE. Yes. I've chosen my life. It isn't going to be divided between a Wall Street office and Newport and Palm Beach. A girl out of a finishing school wouldn't be of any use to me. I'm going to stay right here in Foxon Falls, Minnie, I've got a real job on my hands, and I need a real woman with special knowledge to help me. I don't mean to say we won't have vacations, and we'll sit down and get our education together. Dr. Jonathan will be the schoolmaster.

MINNIE. It's a dream, George.

GEORGE. Well, Minnie, if it's a dream worth dying for it's a dream worth living for. Your brother Bert died for it.

CURTAIN

The End

www.ingramcontent.com/pod-product-compliance
Lightning Source LLC
Chambersburg PA
CBHW072329290526
45794CB00002B/798